LEON: A LIFE

"**This is a wonderful book and a fun read!** Leon has such a distinct voice and it feels so authentic, while at the same time having this quality of larger-than-life storytelling that made me think of the German term *Seemannsgarn*, or seaman's yarn, meaning that sailors spin stories that might be a bit exaggerated. And his wife, Tamara, sounds like a fierce pioneer in her own right. What a great job preserving these stories of such an adventurous life! There are some amazing lines that just made me stop to let them sink in, and some historical aspects that were so interesting to see through his eyes. And of course I laughed a lot!"

        Dr. Joela Jacobs
        University of Arizona

"**LEON: A LIFE** is really many lives packed into **one freewheeling memoir**: the irrepressible Leon Schneider as everything from a busboy and a construction worker to a merchant marine and an actor—and always ready for another adventure. From running after nickels during the Depression to swimming away from U-Boats in World War II: it's all here and all told in a rapid-fire patter that gives us the essence of the man."

        David Galef
        Creative Writing Program Director, Montclair State University.
        Author of *My Date with Neanderthal Woman*

"**LEON: A LIFE** springs from a labor of love: Ivan Schneider, Leon's son, in collaboration with Tamara Schneider, Leon's wife, faithfully recorded the wealth of rollicking memoirs recounted by the 97-year-old Leon. It did not require cajoling: Leon's story bursts forth eagerly, with **riveting humor, raunchy resilience and originality** in the face of circumstances which might have easily defeated others. In addition, there is a nuanced implicit undercurrent of decrying the consequences of ethnic and economic discrimination. For the reader, the book is a treat, with much to admire and to enjoy."

        Lora Heims Tessman
        Author of *The Analyst's Analyst Within* and
        Children of Parting Parents

LEON: A LIFE

THE TRUE STORIES OF CAPTAIN LEON H SCHNEIDER

AS TOLD TO
IVAN SCHNEIDER
the second of
his acknowledged
three children
with the artist
Tamara Schneider

Copyright © 2019 by Ivan Schneider

All Rights Reserved. No part of this book may be reproduced or utilized in any form or by any means, electronic or mechanical, including photocopying, recording, or by any information storage and retrieval system, without permission in writing from the publisher.

ISBN-13: 978-1-7339976-0-7
ISBN-13: 978-1-7339976-1-4 (eBook)

OLD CONVINCER PUBLISHING
An imprint of Taelyen LLC
113 Cherry St. #9495 Seattle, Washington 98104
www.oldconvincer.com

First printing May 2019

Book design by Tamara Schneider
All photographs used by permission of Leon H Schneider

LEON: TABLE OF CONTENTS

- **i** **Introduction** Leon on screen.
- **iii** **Acknowledgements** A family project. Content warnings.
- **1** **Miss Koral** The couple's engagement.
- **2** **Koral–Schneider** Announcement of a simple wedding.
- **4** **Aground and dismasted** West New York. Kingston. Jobs ashore.
- **7** **Overheard** Earliest memories.
- **9** **Arnold** The biggest schmuck in the entire family.
- **11** **The little momzer** Pennies from Pop.
- **12** **Florence** A musical education.
- **13** **Seeing** The eye patch. Mr. Fishman the optician.
- **15** **Craps** The neighborhood game with Cockeyed Sam the newspaper man.
- **17** **Nickels** Stealing and hustling for small change.
- **19** **The neighborhood** Jews and Italians.
- **21** **The bicycle gonif** Leon's new bicycle.
- **23** **The Great Depression** WPA. Selling potatoes and onions.
- **25** **Bar-mitzvah** Three brothers, two bar-mitzvahs.
- **26** **Mom** Leon's yiddishe momme.
- **27** **Mary Gordon** Honoring our Scottish benefactor.
- **27** **Uncle Max** The family matchmaker. The family's first divorce.
- **29** **Kosher Sam** The Orthodox cousins keep their distance.
- **30** **Sonia** Leon's little sister.
- **31** **Muriel** Leon's first crush.
- **32** **Harlem** Leon the jitterbug.
- **34** **Clubhouse** Spin the records, spin the bottle.

35	**The overcoat**	High-school dropout hitchhikes to Florida.
37	**Miami Beach**	Beach jobs. Milton Berle's jokes.
39	**Homeward**	A driver's license and a gas can.
40	**The hunchback**	Delivering dresses. A job for Pop.
41	**Chickens**	Plucking pinfeathers.
42	**Brookside Manor**	Waiting tables in the Catskills.
44	**Up the ranks**	The neighborhood kids join the Navy. Leon goes upstate.
47	**Hollywood and Vine**	Driving to Las Vegas. Anti-Semitism in Los Angeles.
50	**Busboy**	Eat at the theater. Dancing girls.
52	**Bessie and Anna**	Leon's L.A. aunts and their husbands.
54	**Wiper**	San Francisco. Leon's first ocean voyages. Hawaii.
58	**Riding the rails**	Leon the hobo. A cold night outside Sparks. Salt Lake City.
60	**Fireman**	Troop transport. First in Melbourne. Set loose in the sweet shop.
62	**Caribbean Sinkings**	Twice torpedoed.
64	**Trinidad**	A hospital stay.
66	**Torpedo Club**	Leon makes it into LIFE magazine.
67	**Tests**	Communists. Getting into Kings Point.
70	**Rules of the Road**	Life at the academy.
73	**Officer**	A diploma for a high-school dropout.
73	**Eleanor**	Leon's celebrity crush.
75	**The Blitz**	A War Bond rally in D.C., and a bit of a do in London.
78	**War Shipping Administration**	The keys to the kingdom.
80	**Victory in Europe**	Post-war Germany.
83	**Putting up the Ritz**	Free to those who can afford it.
84	**Relief and Rehabilitation**	Leon in charge. A deceitful date.
87	**Japan**	Geisha girls and devastation.

88 **War Bride** A Frenchwoman on a freighter.
89 **Rosita** A romance in Buenos Aires with Rosie the dancer.
90 **Grrrrammi** On a Greek coal-burning freighter to Uruguay.
93 **Invention** Herr Schnapp. Rosie's story.
96 **Refugee** A nice Jewish girl meets a peddler.
97 **Pesos** A rich American in Buenos Aires.
99 **Poor Alfredo** A high-class Uruguayan and his stunning girlfriend.
101 **Deckhand** The Philippines.
103 **Exodus** Leon and the Jewish underground.
105 **Israel** Leon's take on Israel-Palestine.
106 **Ireland** Queen Elizabeth's linen napkins.
107 **Yugoslavia** The ballet dancer.
108 **Korea** A twenty-three-course meal.
109 **Convent** Encounter at the Palace.
110 **Law School** A tricky knot for Leon.
111 **GI Bill** Our ungrateful Congress.
113 **Suez Canal** Jewish sailors in Egypt.
116 **Anka** A message for the fans.
117 **Ocean Avenue** The pains of subletting.
118 **Flatbush** The floating craps game.
120 **Passings** Arnold. Pop.
121 **The Old Convincer** The bridge tour. A day at the beach.
123 **That's it** How I met your mother.
125 **Seventeen's your point** A working woman and a stay-at-home dad.
126 **Extra** In the Screen Actors Guild.
128 **Pensioner** The secret to longevity.

INTRODUCTION

You've seen Leon before. Walking next to Owen Wilson in *The Royal Tenenbaums*.[1] A few steps behind Jack Nicholson in *As Good As It Gets*.[2] Enrobed as a judge in *Law & Order*.

Spend any time with Leon, and you'll hear the rat-tat-tat of jokes, followed by more jokes. Mostly dick jokes. Then you'll hear a story that you think is going to be a joke but turns out to be a real story. While you're reeling from the impact, he tells another joke, and then another story that seems to be real but turns out to be a joke.

But for some inexplicable reason, in his 28-year career as a member of the Screen Actors Guild, Leon has never had a speaking role.

That ends now.

---

[1] The "Eli Cash" scene at the book reading.

[2] The "OCD" scene on the sidewalk.

"I do not doubt that he got some of the story wrong, and that I get some of the story wrong. I will never mistake my memory of my father for my knowledge of him. But I am his heir, not his historian."

- Leon Wieseltier, *Kaddish*

ACKNOWLEDGEMENTS

This is not a family history.

If this were a family history, I'd have to find out more about my grandparents. David Schneider (1879-1966) came to the United States at the age of 14. Alone, he earned enough money selling lamp oil to pay transatlantic passage for his younger siblings, Sam, Anna, and Bessie, and for his parents, Herman and Anna, who lived in Bridgeport, Connecticut until they died in the 1918 flu epidemic. I'd have to find out more about my grandmother Mary Gordon (1892-1980), her brothers Sam and Max, and her parents Esther Hannah Gordon and Isaiah Gordon (d. 1931).

If this were a family history, I'd have to track down the family of Leon's older brother Arnold (1919-1964), who served in the Navy during WWII; and get a full account from my dear Aunt Sonia (b. 1934).

If this were a family history, I'd have to devote entire volumes to Uncle Henry and Aunt Florence.

Florence (1920-2009) graduated from Hunter College. In 1942, she married Charles Adams, a Merchant Marine engineer. After the war, Charles joined the U.S. State Department, and Florence accompanied him throughout his entire career as a Foreign Service Officer. With postings in France, Germany, Morocco, Senegal, Ghana and elsewhere, they had six children born in six different countries.

Henry (b. 1926), upon graduating from Cornell, joined the nascent Central Intelligence Agency, learned to speak Russian, and retired in the 1980s to enjoy with his family a waterfront home, a pair of Vermont ski chalets, and a sailboat named *Odyssey*.

To all of the children of David and Mary, I have the deepest admiration for your service to the United States, humble respect for your principled politics, and lasting gratitude for your gentle love and patient encouragement over the years.

At 97, my father retains his excellent memory. To the best of my recollection, these stories are structurally and materially the same as when I heard them for the first time, or the second time, or the hundredth time; and to the best of my knowledge, they are true stories. Unless we're talking about anything illegal, in which case we made it all up.

The stories in this volume are largely based on interviews conducted in January 2019, along with some recordings from 2013.

Following a few introductory chapters, I have arranged my father's stories in close to chronological order, starting with his earliest memory, and ending, as a comedy should, with a marriage.

My mother, Tamara Schneider, was present for every one of our recording sessions. She is responsible for all the graphics and layout, and also collaborated with me on the editing.

My brother, Eric, scanned the negatives and photos for high-resolution printing, ensuring that we would have a worthy keepsake to distribute at his son's bar-mitzvah.

My sister, Greta, was foremost among the readers I had in mind for this collection. More than anyone, she has the right to hear the whole story, including the parts usually told only to the boys.

While I have made some edits for clarity, I retain the rhythm of the spoken style, with its repetitions, interpolated dialogue, gleeful profanity, and yes, the jokes.

This work is for mature audiences only. Coarse or crude language. Sexual situations. Violence. This is not for Papa Leon's grandchildren, at least until the bar-mitzvah or Sweet Sixteen party, as the case may be.

A note on racial epithets: Leon tells a story about a torpedo attack on his ship. He is blinded and latches onto a man who leads him to safety. He retells the story in way that uses the language of the 1940s: "And there was a Negro messman walked by me..." I include it in the record precisely as spoken, along with the contextual use of the Yiddish *shvartzes*, with my assurance to the reader that these do not, and would not, cover up any uglier slur. I wish to express gratitude to the American merchant mariner who saved my father's life that evening.

A note on offensive language: In this work, you will find instances of disturbing language, anecdotes, and attitudes involving women, gay men, transgender people, people with disabilities, and people of various nationalities and religious affiliations. Even if not spoken with malice, such words still cause pain. My aim in this compilation is not to glorify, but rather to make visible, the language that shaped me and my siblings. The path to reconciliation starts with the truth, and this is it.

A note on prostitution: Sex work should be decriminalized, sex work is not human trafficking, and FOSTA-SESTA should be repealed. No apologies, therefore, are forthcoming for the whorehouse stories.

"I wasn't born when that happened," my mother would say.

Or, "I was just a schoolgirl at the time, it doesn't count."

My mother is the hero of the story. She recognized the kindness, loyalty, and generosity of Leon's spirit, and made everything possible for our family.

Ivan Schneider
April 9, 2019
Seattle, Washington

LEON ON THE SS UNITED STATES

MISS KORAL

Tamara Koral lived in a rent-controlled, one-bedroom, 8th-floor apartment on the Upper West Side.

At first, her younger sister lived with her, but the sister soon went back to their hometown of Kingston, a town in northeast Pennsylvania across the Susquehanna River from the city of Wilkes-Barre.

In 1964, Tamara joined a college friend on a cruise and met Leon in a Bermuda nightclub. They started a long-distance relationship. He'd be gone for months, but Tamara didn't mind. "I had a job and a very busy life, so I could deal with it," she said. "Besides, I liked him."

In 1965, Tamara's sister married a young man in the garment industry, and her parents hosted a large wedding celebration.

By 1967, Tamara was planning to break it off with Leon unless things changed. He returned from a trip with the same thought: "I'd better marry her, or she's going to take off."

They announced their engagement. Her parents didn't quite understand what Leon did for a living or why Tamara was interested in an older man.

Leon and Tamara had planned to go to City Hall. Her parents, relenting without approving, insisted upon a rabbi. They drove to Manhattan, paid for the ceremony in the rabbi's study, and treated the newlyweds to a steak dinner.

KORAL–SCHNEIDER

May 28, 1967 — Miss Tamara Koral, daughter of Mr. Charles Koral and Mrs. Anita Koral of Kingston, Pa., was married this afternoon to Leon H Schneider, son of Mrs. Mary Schneider.

The twenty-dollar ceremony was performed by a rabbi at the Stephen Wise Free Synagogue in Manhattan.

The bride attended Kingston High School and is an avid reader who plays the piano. She earned a Bachelor of Arts in Design from Carnegie Tech in Pittsburgh and works as a paste-up artist at *Seventeen* magazine in New York City. Her parents, Mr. and Mrs. Charles Koral, own a clothing factory in Edwardsville, Pa. and a retail outlet on Market Street in Kingston.

The groom is a 1944 graduate of Kings Point U.S. Merchant Marine Academy and received his unlimited master's license in 1956. He began sailing in 1941, and during World War II, he was on two merchant ships sunk by German U-Boats, and worked for the War Shipping Administration in London. Leon is from Brooklyn. The groom's father, the late Mr. David Schneider, passed away last year at the age of 87, and his widow, Mrs. Mary Schneider, lives in Brooklyn.

The marriage ceremony was witnessed by the bride's parents, the bride's younger sister, and her sister's husband.

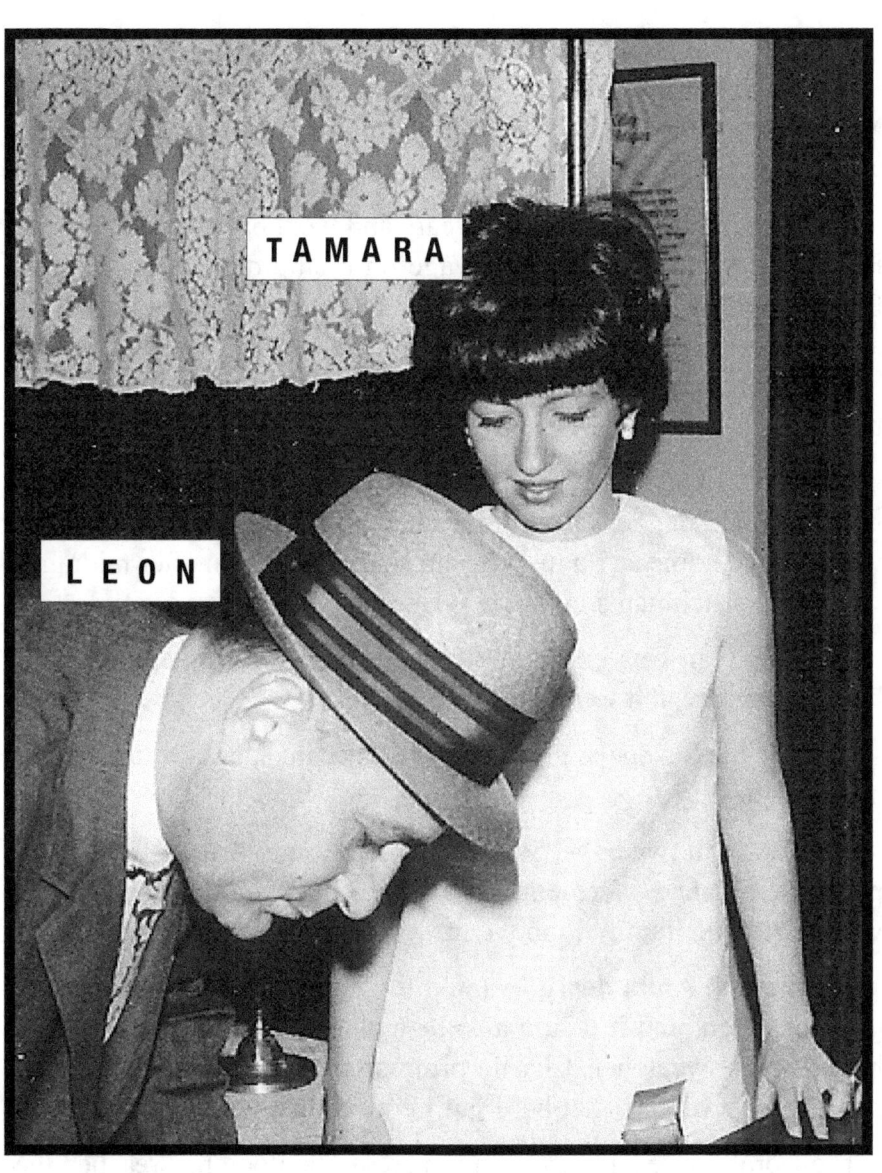

AGROUND AND DISMASTED

Leon and Tamara rented an apartment together in West New York, New Jersey. They quickly learned that Tamara was pregnant. Eric was born prematurely that December at 5 lbs, 3 oz.

In 1968, Tamara put Eric in daycare and went back to work, while Leon took his final working voyage on a ship delivering supplies for the military in Vietnam. When he returned, Leon studied to be a registered stockbroker and was hired at Merrill Lynch, but in the bear market that followed, the best he could do was sell telephone bonds.

He soon took a second job, working the four-to-midnight shift as a security guard on the waterfront, catnapping between his rounds. He would leave home at 7 a.m. wearing a suit and return after midnight wearing a watchman's uniform.

In 1970, Ivan was born. After maternity leave, Tamara put both boys in daycare and went back to work.

In 1972, the Susquehanna overflowed its banks, flooding Kingston and Wilkes-Barre.

In 1973, with two boys, 5 and 2, Tamara found that she was again pregnant. Finances were tenuous. Tamara consulted with her parents, who invited the family to move in with them.

Charlie and Anita dearly wanted to spend more time with their grandchildren, and it would also be a chance to get to know Leon better. As a sweetener, Charlie promised, or maybe suggested, or possibly just hinted, that he'd put Leon in business.

The Koral house had just been repaired. The flood had reached the second floor, and then two feet above the second floor. Charlie and Anita slept in a HUD trailer in an adjacent lot. Leon and Tamara took the bedroom on the second floor, and Eric and Ivan slept in the attic.

Under the same roof, Leon and Charlie "were like two bulls

facing one another," recalls Tamara. Words were exchanged. Leon suggested they step outside, to which Charlie replied: "You wanna *fight* me? What, are you crazy?"

Tamara knew that it was time for them to move. They found a nearby home for sale for $30,000, sanitized after the flood but still needing work. Charlie refused to help with the ten-percent down payment. Leon called his brother Henry and said, "Lend me three thousand dollars and I'll paint your house." Henry accepted the deal, and the house was purchased. Greta was born later that year.

The promised business never materialized for Leon. Shortly thereafter, Tamara's brother, David, came back from California. Charlie started him off in business, and David thrived in Kingston.

Leon did not thrive in Kingston.

He enjoyed only one job during his time there, and that was teaching celestial navigation to adult education students at Luzerne County Community College in Nanticoke, Pa. He taught the students how to find due south using a wristwatch, and about latitude and longitude, the North Star, the Southern Cross. He told jokes, many jokes. One man enjoyed the class so much that he took it again along with his 12-year-old daughter, which pained Leon because he could no longer tell most of his jokes.

Leon had his union pension of $5,000 per year, but it was not indexed to inflation and not enough to support a family of five.

Leon rejoined Merrill Lynch at its Wilkes-Barre office, working on commission. He prospected and cold-called with meager results. After nine months, Leon quit.

Leon was a print shop salesman, working on commission. Leon and Tamara had a favorable meeting with the managers of a department store in Allentown and prepared to bid on designing and printing their flyers. The owner of the print shop demurred, saying that his small outfit didn't have the high-volume web press needed to fulfill the large daily order. Discouraged and unable to make a living in this manner, Leon quit.

Leon was a car salesman, working on commission. The auto dealership was in a building fronted with 25-foot-high glass windows. An elderly couple entered the dealership in tears having been sold a lemon. The owner's son pointed to the 25-foot-high glass windows. "Look at those windows," he said. "Do you see any stained glass? This is not a church!"

Leon answered the phone at the auto dealership. On the line was the print shop owner, who recognized Leon's voice. "You remember that department store? I bought the printing press and I got the job," he said.

"I don't recall getting my commission," replied Leon.

"That's what I like about you, Leon," said the print shop owner. "You always had a great sense of humor."

One day, a man entered the auto dealership. Leon showed the man some vehicles and accompanied him on test drives. The man bought a car that very day. The owner's son then claimed that the man was an acquaintance of his, and therefore his own customer, denying Leon the commission. Leon quit.

And then, Captain Leon H Schneider, USMMA '44, master of vessels, all ships, diesel or steam, of any size, upon any ocean, decorated with the Merchant Marine Mariner's Medal and two-time member of the Torpedo Club, took a job at the Wyoming Valley Mall. He managed a store for ladies' clothing, and he worked 12 hours a day, seven days a week. In the shop across the corridor worked the mother of his wife's sister's husband. The mall being practically empty at all times, she called upon Leon often, bearing the latest tidings of the extended family of his wife's sister's husband, day upon day.

"Marchant service indeed! I suppose now ye feel considerable proud of having served in those marchant ships." – Herman Melville, *Moby-Dick*

OVERHEARD

Uncle Sam wanted sons.

Hannah is crying to my mother. Sam and Hannah have two daughters. No sons. He's pissed at her. He started cheating on her. He went out to California once with this nurse, he was banging this nurse.

That was Uncle Sam, Pop's younger brother.

I was in the crib at the time. It's amazing how you can remember something when you're in a crib.

My mother lost most of her hearing in childhood. One winter, she crashed her sled into a tree. I started speaking loudly so that my mother could hear me.

She got a primitive hearing aide. The battery attached to her leg, and a four-inch microphone was on a little string hanging down from her neck. When I spoke to her, I spoke to the midpoint of her chest so that she would hear me.

– Not so loudly, it hurts my ears.

ARNOLD

My brothers were always the smart ones. I was the putz.

Arnold was three years older than me. When I took a bath, he'd come in and sink my boats. He torpedoed my navy.

Arnold was such a pussy. He was a first-rate engineer. When World War II started, he went into the Navy, and he could have been an officer in 90 days. They were looking for engineering graduates. He didn't accept a commission because it would have meant going out of town and leaving his dear Shirley, his goddamn cockamamie sick bride, the only woman he ever knew.

My sister introduced them when they were in grade school. They stayed together and got married.

She never went to any of our family's affairs. Only her family. — Oh, we can't go. — Oh, the boys have their violin lessons. Always an excuse. Arnold went to our cousin's child's bar-mitzvah, he went alone, she wouldn't even go with him. He writes a ten-dollar check. Later, she says — You gave ten dollars and you didn't ask me? She stopped payment on the check. Naturally, the whole family knew about Shirley's dereliction, and Arnold the wuss. That made my brother the biggest schmuck in the entire family.

If it was me, I would have thrown her in the street and said — Go back to your father and mother, because we're through. You made a schmuck out of me to my entire family? You are now a schmuck-*ess*. OUT!

But he took it, he took it. He abandoned the family, dumped us while we were still in the Depression, so he could go and fuck Shirley the cunt. When he graduated as a mechanical engineer, we were still suffering from the Depression, we're barely surviving. I always held this against him. We were eating shit, all of us. In an Italian family, the oldest son wouldn't even go to college, he would stay with the family and help support the siblings. Arnold, the day he graduated, he married Shirley and left the house. He got married, he's not giving us any money.

Any money that I earned as a kid, I used to bring home, I'd give my mother the money and she went out and bought bread with it. I was helping my parents when I wasn't stealing from them.

THE LITTLE MOMZER

Pop used to whack me around a lot, because I used to steal from his little wallet with the pennies in it. I'd sneak in and take some money out. I stole from my father to go out and buy food. Or maybe gamble with it. I started shooting craps at the age of six.

One day he started to beat the shit out of me, but I hadn't taken anything that time.

He's running after me — you took money from my wallet, I'll get you, you little *momzer* — which is Yiddish for bastard.

I climbed under the bed. He pulled the whole bed away. I'm exposed like a fucking rat. He used to shave with a straight-edge razor. He had a strop. The strop was what he used to whack me on the ass. This was one fucking weapon.

He had an accident to his thumb, but he was too cheap to go to a doctor. It became infected. Gangrene set in. He had to go to a doctor, and they had to cut off half his thumb, so he spent the rest of his life with half a thumb.

He had to give up the straight-edge razor, because you have to use the thumb as a guide. Picture trying to hold a straight-edge razor with no thumb. He started using safety blades, but he wouldn't buy blades. They were a penny each then. He'd take out the blade, rub the little blade on this emery stone, put it back in the razor and shave with that. He'd use the same blade 88 times. That was Pop.

FLORENCE

We used to move every three to six months because in the Depression days, they would give you the first month free. Concession, it was called.

One place had a piano, so my older sister started learning to play the piano.

And then she went to Erasmus High, where Florence played the clarinet. They loaned her a clarinet. One day she was in an auto accident. She fell out of the car, she's lying in the street. And the ambulance came. But while she's lying in the street, somebody stole her clarinet. You know people – opportunists. She went back to school — sorry we can't give you another one, you had it, that's it.

Six months later, the doorbell rings.

I was a little *gonif* then, I was a little thieving fuck. I didn't miss a chance.

The doorbell rings. I look down, I recognize two detectives, these two big burly goyim. I figure — oh shit what did I do?

They look up.

—Does Schneider live here?

—Yeah.

—Florence Schneider?

—Yeah.

What the fuck could she have done?

Somebody had pawned her clarinet. The detectives had the number on the clarinet and took it away from the pawnshop and returned it to her. Six months later, my sister got her clarinet back.

SEEING

When I was six years old, the doctor says to my parents — you should patch his good eye.

My left eye was bad. They put the patch on my good eye.

—I don't like it.

If I had covered the good eye, the lazy eye would have been forced to work, and I wouldn't have had such a bad eye. Americanized parents would have said — You have to wear it if you want your eye to get better.

My parents were immigrants, they don't know.

—Eh, don't wear it.

At that age, I used to ride the subways alone. Today, a 15-year-old kid, you have to take them by the hand to cross the street. I'm six years old and my parents gave me a nickel each way for the subway.

I went to Mr. Fishman. Technically he wasn't allowed to examine my eyes. He wasn't an ophthalmologist. He was only an optician. But Mr. Fishman examined eyes anyway. He was our neighbor, he lived on the same street. I rode to Manhattan, he examined my eyes, and he made a prescription – examination, eye glasses and frames, five dollars.

He's examining my eyes.

—What do you see?

—I see your mouthwash isn't working.

Ninety years ago, I was a ball breaker. Imagine that.

For five dollars I got glasses, frames, and an exam. And then I went around the corner and got a five-cent haircut. This was a barber college, where all the Tonys were learning their trade, and the master barber would go around saying — Hey Joe, cut a little here, cut a little there.

I got a nickel haircut and five-dollar glasses, and then I put a nickel on the subway and went home.

CRAPS

We used to shoot craps on the railroad sidings in the neighborhood, on weekends when there were no trains running. All the railroad platforms were occupied. There were about thirty crap games going.

The whole neighborhood was shooting craps, the kids with their pennies, the big-times with their dollars. And occasionally the cops would come, throw their club at the whole group, the club would come bouncing in, hit somebody in the ass, we'd all run away, and then the cops would come in and pick up the money. One cop had a club with "Kosher" written on it. The son of a bitch.

I was a newsboy for Cockeyed Sam, he had a glass eye. I was maybe eight or nine. I used to sell papers until midnight, so I slept in school.

I used to sell newspapers for 50 cents a night. People would buy a *News* and *Mirror* for two cents each, they'd give you a nickel. And sometimes they'd even give you a dime.

Sam says — The tips are mine. Because it's my route. You're working for me.

He used to search the kids when they left to make sure they didn't have any money. When I worked for 50 cents a night, my tips I used to put in a jockstrap that I wore. Eight years old, you could buy a small jock, or I put on a tight bathing suit or something. He'd look in my pockets, but he wouldn't look at my prick, right?

He had all of Flatbush Avenue in Brooklyn. Five spots selling newspapers every night — *News, Mirror, American, Times, Tribune, Eagle*. He used to make a lot of money.

Cockeyed Sam was a big gambler. He didn't bet nickels and dimes. He had a bankroll. He was always a right better, and he would bet a lot.

But I knew one thing Sam didn't know. When Sam played, they would throw phony dice in, to make the dice miss. I knew that, so when Sam played, I used to go to the game he was in, and bet with the betters, wrong.

There was one guy with long skinny fingers and he was the expert crap shooter. What he would do – he'd roll out the kosher dice, which were good, and then when he'd pick them up, he'd have phony dice in his hand. He would swap it in for the good dice. It would always come up seven.

I'd bet against Sam, and I used to make more money shooting craps than I made from his 50 cents a night.

This guy with the long skinny fingers, he's playing with the heavyweights now and he's still pulling that shit. He had the two dice, and he had to substitute one for the other using his fingers. He fucked up, and three dice rolled out.

They said – Keep rolling buddy. Thirteen's your point.

Then they broke his fingers. They broke his fucking fingers. I didn't see him around anymore.

NICKELS

The newsstand was outside the candy store. People used to pick up their *News*, and it was two cents each. Or they'd pick up a *News* and a *Mirror* and leave a nickel on the counter. They didn't bother going into the store.

I'd walk by and look around and I'd grab the nickels. I'd steal their money off the newsstands.

Whenever I'd pass a fruit market with the displays outside with the oranges and apples, boy was I fast.

Listen, we had to survive in those days. Five kids and a grandparent living in a room the size of this table.

No refrigerators. Women would shop every day because they couldn't keep food overnight. Anything you wanted to keep, you put into an aluminum box outside the window, tied with picture wire. Sometimes people would put milk out in the box. I used to sneak around and grab the milk bottles. Steal the milk from my neighbors. I didn't give a shit. There was a little courtyard with all the buildings around it. I'd grab a bottle of milk, drink it, and bring it back and get three cents deposit.

I was a little *gonif*, and that's how you survived.

Nobody had a phone in those days, because it cost money. The candy store had a phone. We hung around the candy store, that was where we met. And if a phone call came in at the candy store—Get Mrs. Ginsburg. She's half a block away. The people on the other end knew they had to wait. So we'd run and get Mrs. Ginsburg, but she had to give us a nickel. That was the rule. If you didn't tip you never got a call. —Fuck you, Mrs. Ginsburg, I'm not going to come to your house.

So we used to run and collect nickels that way.

In Borough Park, 13th Avenue looked like the Lower East Side, if you recall pictures of that, the peddlers with the pushcarts, guys walking around selling garlic. That's where I sold shopping bags. I used to buy 50 shopping bags for 50 cents and put them in the closet. I'd go down there with a handful and sell them for two cents each. So everybody bought two shopping bags, doubled them up, and gave me a nickel.

I remember this one lady stopping me and she says—oh, *ze kalte*—it's cold. She buttoned my shirt, and I remember her saying—oh such a *sheyne boychik*—a very pretty boy.

I was an attractive little boy. Riding the subway, a lot of queers used to come up to me. I'm eight, nine years old on the subway.

—Get the fuck outta here.

I knew the language.

Now if one of them wanted to pay me a dollar to give me a blowjob, that would have been a different story. A dollar was big money in those days. For fifteen cents you could go for Chinese and get egg drop soup, chow mein, rice, and after that a pineapple and a fortune cookie.

THE NEIGHBORHOOD

We ended up in a four-room apartment in a skinny row house. And the row houses each were 20 feet wide, like a railroad flat. You'd walk in, and that was the end of it. You didn't see any daylight or anything. But we did have a back window, which reached out into a little grass garden. I used to jump into the garden and catch little grasshoppers and pull their legs off.

The last time I saw Borough Park, I was shocked. What used to be a nice neighborhood, Jewish on one side, Italians across the street, it's all ultra-Orthodox Jews running around. It happened to be a Jewish holiday, so me driving even through there, if they knew I was Jewish, they would have pelted the car. They're all walking around in their *shabbos* garb, and I said — What the hell happened to my nice Borough Park? Used to be nice, Italians and Jews, and that was it.

We used to fight the kids across the street. Johnny was the older brother, Frankie was a young guy, and he and I used to fistfight. Many years later, I'm riding the subway, and the older brother Johnny was on it. this was 20 years later, but I have a memory for faces. I even remember the time his mother died, I remember what his mother looked like. Would you believe it? I was going to go across to say something. I didn't bother. I didn't want to shock the guy.

THE BICYCLE GONIF

I was ten years old, selling newspapers on the corner in Brooklyn. I saved a quarter at a time, and when I had ten dollars, I went out and bought a bike. It was a beautiful bike, a Silver King with inflated balloon tires. It was a hundred-dollar bike, but I got it for ten dollars, so it was probably stolen. Nobody could sell a bike like that for ten dollars.

I'm riding home and think — I'd better get a lock and a chain.

So I rode to the local Sears Roebuck, and rather than leave it outside, I dragged it down two flights of stairs to the hardware department and went to buy a chain. I turn around and the bike was gone. It was the biggest loss of my life.

My father would never believe that I had a bike for ten minutes and somebody already stole it. He would have blamed me for losing the ten dollars in a crap game or a poker game. I couldn't go home without a bike.

I took a subway to the Bronx. There were agencies that rented bikes for fifty cents for the day, but you needed an ID.

I'm such a smart little prick at ten years old. I went into a local apartment building, picked out a name, and went to the local Public Service building.

—My mother lost her bill, she needs a bill for this name and address.

They gave me a bill. I crumpled it up, put it in my pocket, and went to the local bike store.

—I want to rent a bike.

—Do you have any ID?

—Yeah, I think I've got this.

I take this crumpled bill out of my pocket, show it to them, and they give me the bike. I pedal it from the Bronx back to Brooklyn.

A year later, I'm selling newspapers on Flatbush Avenue, and the bike is chained next to the light fixture. A car pulls up to buy a newspaper. Two guys get out.

—That's our bike. Where did you get it?

—I bought it.

—It's our bike. We're calling the police.

—No, I don't want any trouble.

They took the bike.

I rode home holding onto the back of the Flatbush trolley. The next morning I started crying. My father said — What's wrong? I said — Somebody stole my bike, they sawed off the lock. That was the end of it.

My father was a bike rider himself, he knew bikes.

—How did you get a brand-new bike for ten dollars?

—Some kid on the block was injured on a bike and so the kid's father said I don't want you to have a bike, and he got rid of it.

I was such a little fucking bastard, you'd think a guy like that would grow up to be the president.

THE GREAT DEPRESSION

My father was the cheapest. All the pressure from years of deprivation made him so that he couldn't spend a nickel. The Depression ruined him. He spent five or six years with five children and his father-in-law with no money. We were literally on the verge of starvation. Nothing to eat unless I personally stole the money.

We never had two spoons that looked alike. We had glassware from the Standard Oil company and from *yahrzeit* candles. All our tableware came from a multimillionaire – Woolworth. We didn't care.

My father was a skilled machine operator, but the factory closed. He was out of work. But if a lamp broke, he would rewire it.

He got on WPA, Works Progress Administration. I used to call it We Pay Always. It was a relief organization, but they didn't hand you a check. You had to work for the 14 dollars a week.

They said — We're going to give you a pick and shovel and we're going to send you out to Floyd Bennett Field — which was a zillion miles from where we lived, for a 35-cents-an-hour job. He took a trolley car for five cents to the end of Coney Island. If you wanted to get to Floyd Bennett Field, you had to spend another five cents. No transfers in those days. He would walk the four miles to save the nickel, and then he'd walk the four miles back.

He'd leave the house at six in the morning, come home late, at eight o'clock at night, and he made 35 cents an hour, $2.80 per day, less ten cents trolley fare. Digging with a pick and shovel for eight hours a day.

On the weekends, he'd rent a horse and wagon for three dollars a day. We would get up in the middle of the night and go to the farmer's market, and he'd buy over a thousand pounds of potatoes for a penny a pound.

We bought paper bags to put the potatoes and onions in, and we bought a sign — POTATOES 18 LBS. FOR A QUARTER.

The A&P was selling for 15 pounds for a quarter, why not buy from the peddler?

I'm 10 or 11 years old, and I would drive the horse and wagon, like I'm in an old-time western. He would yell — Potatoes, Potatoes and Onions! Eighteen pounds for a quarter!

Then he got a taxi and he fixed it up like a truck, so that he could sell the potatoes and onions from the back of the truck. He used to let me drive. I learned how to shift, and I would drive very slowly in low gear. But he wouldn't let me cross the intersection. He'd walk on the sidewalk while I'm driving the truck.

We used to pick up some rocks with the potatoes and put them in with it too. Also, you'd have a heavy thumb on the scale. But people were smart, they had their own scales.

Someone would say — Bring me up 18 pounds. I'd bring up 15 pounds.

They'd say — Hey, it's 15 pounds —Sorry, I must be off. I'd have to run downstairs, make it 18 pounds, go back upstairs.

At the end of the day we made three or four dollars, and we used to eat a lot of leftover potatoes and onions. We lived on potatoes. I love potatoes today.

I liked being with my father. We'd stop off and we'd get pea soup at this place. It was the most wonderful dish I'd ever had in my life. I used to remember this particular pea soup was like nectar. I would lap that up. We didn't have bacon in the house, but we'd go out and he let me have bacon and ham and all that shit.

BAR-MITZVAH

I never was bar-mitzvah'd because it cost a dollar a week for the rabbi, and I didn't have the dollar. It was 1934, and Pop was getting 14 dollars a week from WPA. He said — Leon, I don't have the dollar a week for the rabbi. So I never got bar-mitzvah'd.

But Arnold and Henry were both bar-mitzvah'd. Henry studied with his friend Marvin who was getting bar-mitzvah'd. Henry picked up what he needed from his friend Marvin. He didn't get a rabbi. Marvin had a rabbi and Marvin used to give Henry the information. That's how my father beat the dollar a week for Henry.

MOM

She used to buy food every day, because without a refrigerator we had to buy it and eat it. Now, when we didn't have the money and the money would come at the end of the week, or the end of the month, the grocer would have a little notebook and would write down what Mrs. Schneider owed, and when she went to buy something, she didn't know from eighths. She knew "a quarter" in Yiddish, a *fertl* was a quarter. She didn't know enough to say one-eighth. She had to say a *halb a fertl* a half of a quarter, if she wanted something like cottage cheese, or a slice of something or other.

She belonged to this Workmen's Circle group. There were about eight or ten women, so every tenth time, they'd meet in our meager little home. And it always pissed my father off, because at these meetings, every woman had to drop a dollar off into the fund to go for some charity for the poor. That was a dollar, that was money in those days. He didn't like it, but my mother ignored him and put the dollar in. I knew all the ladies, they all used to talk to me when they visited. I knew them all, all the ladies knew me.

I never remember her being dressed up. She was a very attractive woman. I saw a picture of a queen or a high-toned princess in Europe, and it was my mother, they looked so much alike. My mother looked so elegant, but she never had makeup, she never had dresses, she never even bought a box of sanitary napkins. I mean, that's how bad things were. No manhole covers. Just old *shmatas* cut up to use once a month.

My father never took her out to the movies because a movie would be no good for her with her hearing. A movie was 10 cents, god forbid. My father wouldn't spend 10 cents. He was so cheap.

He never took her out for dinner. Ever. Ever. Ever.

MARY GORDON

Her name was Miriam Gordon. I don't know how it became Mary.

Gordon is an old Scottish name. There was a town in Europe, a shtetl where all the Jews lived, and at the time it was under the directorate of the British Empire. They had a Major Gordon there who was a very benevolent man, a good man. He didn't oppress the shtetl Jews. When the Jews from that shtetl came to America, they were asked — What's your name? They all said — Gordon.

UNCLE MAX

When my father was in Bridgeport, he had a grocery store. There was a whorehouse upstairs. My father used to visit, I know that, he mentioned the whorehouse once. —OK, Pa, say no more.

That was before he met my mother. Uncle Max introduced them.

Max visited my father's grocery store to sell him a refrigerator. He started talking to Dave Schneider, found out he was single and said – I have a sister. Want a nice girl? Have I got a girl for you.

I used to work for Uncle Max for fifty cents a day. He would pick me up in the morning when I was seven or eight years old. I'd open up a can of Noxon and polish all the chrome on the refrigerators. And he used to give me a quarter to go up and get a quart of Breyer's ice cream. We didn't have that kind of money to buy ice cream. Uncle Max was OK with me.

Uncle Max had a wealthy, American-born wife. Minnie was an elegant-looking woman with pince-nez glasses, spoke beautiful English. It was Max and Minnie.

He ran through a lot of her money. All of these different businesses, and they all flopped, so finally she said, no more money, Max, and so he met a rich widow.

In my family, there were no divorces. People married, and whether they liked it or not they were married. A divorce? It was a big shame.

Max was the first one. But she refused to go along with the divorce. He got an out-of-state divorce, which was not legal in New York. This meant he had to stay in New Jersey. If he came to New York and she knew about it, she could have him arrested as a bigamist.

He was still married to her, but she would not give it up — You want to divorce me? I won't accept a divorce. Do what you want to do.

He married this rich widow and started in on her money. He was a very attractive man, always driving a nice Oldsmobile or Buick.

He went ahead and bought some property with four or five dwellings and it looked like a big money-loser. Then, the state decided to build this major highway right alongside it. Suddenly, he became very wealthy. That property went out of sight. Now that he was a very rich, he became part of the *shul* and used to make donations. He was so free and easy with the money once he made it.

His second wife said — My husband Max is such a genius.

When he died, I went to the service. There were 12 rabbis sitting up there. That must have been a lot of contributions. They spoke about Max and made him into a saint, my Uncle Max.

KOSHER SAM

Max's older brother Sam was a real prick.

We only saw Sam once or twice in my life, because he was very kosher, and we were not kosher. My mother would buy kosher meat from the local guy, but if I wanted a glass of milk with my hamburger, she'd give me a glass of milk. She used to clean up at Passover, but Sam knew she wasn't really kosher, and he was Orthodox. One of these religious bullshit artists. He would never visit because God forbid he'd be in a non-kosher home.

We never got to know our first cousins. Although years later, I bought a used Mercedes. We were driving home from Connecticut, and something happened to the rubber on the windshield wiper, and the bare metal scratched up the windshield. We had to pull over and wait until the rain stopped. It was going to cost $800 to put in a new windshield, but I heard about this outfit in Warwick, N.Y. that would remove scratches. I got on the phone and made an appointment, and then I said — You know, I had a cousin in Warwick who I haven't seen in 40 years, his name is Seymour Gordon. He said — You're speaking to Seymour Gordon. We became good friends.

But I only saw Sam twice, and I had no use for the guy because he ignored his own sister.

SONIA

When my sister was born in 1934, my mother was in her late forties. It was an accident, they didn't need another child. So my Uncle Max, who was childless, offered to adopt her. But my mother turned him down. That was her brother, Uncle Max.

MURIEL

I was madly in love at 12 years old. Her name was Muriel. She was a beauty. I used to ride my bike to the street she lived just to get a look at her after school, and oh, she looked like Elizabeth Taylor. We were in the same class, she never knew I was alive.

Years later, I was home visiting, and I'm walking by and there's a woman in front of me with a big fat ass, pushing a baby carriage with a couple children. I walked by and it was Muriel. Oh my God, she got fat. I should have stopped and just chatted with her and said – I knew you in junior high school, but you never knew me.

I was madly in love with her. Never spoke to her, she never spoke to me. As I said, she got fat and had kids. That was the end of Muriel.

HARLEM

When I was 15, I used to get on the subway for a nickel and ride to 125th Street, and get off, and go to the Apollo Theater. I'd ride up, it took me an hour to get to Harlem.

I loved the music. I was a jitterbug in those days, and these were all the great Black musicians. It was 50 cents to get into the Apollo, and I sat there in the balcony and you've got all Black people, and one white little 15-year-old shit sitting there. And I used to listen to all the great bands – Cab Calloway, Jimmie Lunceford, Duke Ellington, Count Basie. I'm trying to remember – I used to know the names of all the drummers and the trumpet players. I loved it.

I didn't fool around after I left the theater, I'm not looking for any action. I'm 15 or 16 years old. I'd walk out, get into the subway, and come home.

I always went alone to Harlem. Except one time I took a girl with me, but she was afraid to go. She went with me, but — oh I'm afraid, the *shvartzes* scare me. There were no Blacks where we lived.

I never had any problem in Harlem. I didn't antagonize anyone, I sat there, listened to the music, and went home.

But oh, when I left the Apollo, I went to a place called the Savoy Ballroom. Now this ballroom had amateur dancers who were better than professionals. They all had jackets, like baseball jackets, and on the back it said The Savoy 400. And I used to go up there, and watch them dance, and then I'd go home and try to imitate what I'd seen. But all these Savoy 400s were fantastic. They were the guys who were throwing women under their legs and over their shoulders and around their whatever. And beautiful dancers. They were jitterbugs like you can't believe. I'd go home and try to remember what they did, try to practice it. I'd go to the Savoy Ballroom, then I'd go home.

I had a good evening. I was alone. I'd watch the dancers, and then I'd try to imitate them. I was a good dancer.

CLUBHOUSE

On our block, everybody lived in a place that had a cellar. So we picked one of the apartments that had a big cellar, and we got a lot of cast-off sofas and furnished the basement, so it was our club. A clubhouse in the basement. And we were all about 15 or 16.

We had a little record player, you'd wind it up. We'd have the record player in the basement of our club, and we'd dance. We invited girls down there, we were 15 and 16 and we used to play kissing games in the basement. You'd sit around, spin the bottle, you know how that plays, don't you?

A group of us sit around in a big circle, alternate he-she-he-she around the circle, and we'd spin the milk bottle, you'd spin it, and where it would stop, at what girl, you and she would go behind the sheets and kiss. And you'd grab a little feel-up, you know, and then we'd go back and sit down, and we'd spin the bottle again. It's amazing that nobody got diseases, everybody kissing everybody. By the end of the evening, you've kissed every girl, you've swapped spit with her. Ah, the good old days.

And there was one girl ... forget about it.

THE OVERCOAT

At first, I went to New Utrecht High School, but then I transferred to a school in New York City called Straubenmuller Textile High School. They had a program whereby you could work a week and go to school a week. That's to keep kids from dropping out during the Depression.

I was at school one week, and the next I worked in Macy's as a stock clerk. I got 35 cents an hour, or 14 dollars a week, every other week. That kept us afloat. I used to bring the money home to my parents. I kept carfare for myself, and lunch money.

It was wintertime, I didn't have an overcoat. I said fuck this and I just quit. I was a goddamn high school dropout at 16.

I told my folks goodbye, and I got on the highway and I hitchhiked down to Florida.

What I did, I went down to the Lincoln Tunnel and I stood outside the tunnel and I looked for trucks with out-of-state licenses. I went up to one truck and said — I'm heading south. He says — Get aboard.

I had no money and no clothes. Just a little bag with a change of underwear and a toothbrush.

A truck here and a truck there.

One car picked me up. A farmer, and he drives into his farm and into his barn, and then he puts his hand on my leg. I said — no I don't go for that crap.

Well look, he was a man and I was a kid, he could have killed me right then and there and you never would have heard from me. But he realized I'm not going in for that crap, so he let me go.

Anyway, that's the hazards of hitchhiking. You pick up a guy and you don't know if he's going to kill you, or you're going to kill him.

But in those days, hitchhiking was an acceptable thing. Today, I would never pick up anybody, I'd be afraid. Lot of nutcases and drug cases, whatever.

MIAMI BEACH

I got to Florida with no money. There were little boxes on the beach where they used to store all the beach chairs, so I climbed in one of them and that's where I slept.

And then I got a job as a busboy. I rented a room run by a woman that used to know my mother in New York. Her name was Mrs. Mintz. And it was 50 cents a night and you'd sleep in the basement on a cot.

She rented the cot to two other guys who were merchant mariners. I didn't know anything about the Merchant Marine then, I was only 17. They took me out at night and we went shrimping. I never ate shrimp, you know, from a Jewish background, and we sat out there with a net and a little light, and you'd see the shrimp going by in the Biscayne Bay. So we scooped them up and had shrimp and went home and cooked them up and ate them. My first fishing experience and also my first shrimp.

I got a job with Mrs. Mintz's sons. They had a concession for beach chairs. All the hotels on the beach would have their chairs stacked up in the back, and when one of the guests wanted a chair, somebody would have to carry the chair for them across the street to the beach. So I got a job delivering chairs. I had to walk across the street, and then they would give me a tip. So I was making nickels and dimes.

But one of the sons wanted to fire me. He says — the kid smells. I had no access to baths. I used to wash up in the gas station, I'd brush my teeth and wash my face. And I was wearing heavy winter pants, I didn't have anything else, and the pants already started to smell. He said — why do you want to keep that kid around, he smells? — Oh give him a break. I cut the pants at the legs. I made a tip here and there, and lived that way.

I worked at an orange juice stand. All the juice you could drink for five cents. I'd cut the oranges, stand there with a hand pump, serve them. A guy would show up and think they're going to drink a gallon. You drink a big glass, you're finished. — Five cents.

I got a busboy job in a restaurant. They paid about 10 dollars a week, which was enough. Then I moved to another busboy job at a nightclub called the Carousel Bar on 21st Street. At the time, Miami Beach ended at 23rd Street. After that it was just beach, nothing. Of course, it became Northern Miami and anybody who had that property became a zillionaire.

At the Carousel, I used to listen to Milton Berle. He was only in his early thirties then. In the front of the nightclub was his mother, along with an outstandingly beautiful former Follies Girl queen. There was no food service during his shtick, so the lights went dark and I stood in the back and listened to all his jokes. I'm still using his jokes.

PAPPY'S MIAMI BEACH RESTAURANT 1939

LEON

HOMEWARD

I got my driver's license in Miami Beach by going to a drugstore on 5th Street and Collins Avenue. The druggist would give you a driver's license, without a test, for 50 cents.

I walked in there and said — I want a driver's license. And he said — Can you drive? And I said — Yes! And he gave me a driver's license.

The way I traveled then, I got one of these gas cans that holds five gallons of gas, not the rectangular one, but a short, round orange-looking thing. I cut a hole in it and I put my underwear and my socks and my toothbrush and toothpaste in the can. I'd walk along the highway carrying the thing, it looks like a motorist out of gas. Some guy would stop and say—where's your car? I say — I have no car, I'm hitchhiking. But when they've already stopped, I've got a ride. That's called gaming the system.

I spent six months in Florida, came home, had a fantastic tan.

The highway rest stops had separate rest rooms for WHITE and COLORED. I'm going in and a little Black boy says to me — Hey Mister, you can't use that one. I say — Son, where I come from, we all piss in the same pot.

THE HUNCHBACK

I was home, and I worked for the hunchback. He started off in life with a pushcart delivering dresses, and he built it up into the Empire Carriers, which had over 20 trucks. We would work on the trucks and get a quarter an hour.

In the afternoons, we started at 1400 Broadway, where all the dress shops were. They would have dresses to be delivered to retail stores. We would run up and down the building, ring the bells and say — Empire Carriers—and they say—come in—and the shipping clerk would give us a box with the address on it. We'd bring it down to the truck, and they would take it to the main building on 39th Street and 12th Avenue, and they would sort it out, and then put them in the proper trucks to go to the Bronx, to Brooklyn, wherever they went.

At night, we would go with the trucks. The truck would stop, you'd drop off a box, and then you'd run after the truck while it made the next stop. I would be running all night dropping boxes off.

Abe was a little guy, a hunchback, and my joke was — Hey, loan me some money and I'll pay you back when Abe straightens out. Terrible joke.

I asked the boss — Can my father work here? — and he says — We only pay these guys thirty-five cents an hour. Well, he's not getting anything, and so my father came down to the place, he wouldn't turn down anything, you know. And so I saw my father on the floor, moving boxes around, oh…I felt terrible. I don't mind working for thirty-five cents an hour, I'm seventeen, but there's the old man dragging shit around. He never got over it, he was depressed the rest of his life.

CHICKENS

That summer, I was hitchhiking and went up to the Catskills. I'm walking along the highway, and a guy stops.

—Where you going?

—I'm looking for a job.

—There's a place, we have a little *kohelain*.

It's do-your-own-cooking, room-and-board place, and he takes me there, and this big fat Jewish woman says — 15 dollars a month, you know how to pluck chickens? I said — Yes! I used to watch my mother pluck the pinfeathers out of the chickens.

So she sits me down with a bunch of dead chickens, and the flies are buzzing around, and I'm plucking chickens and she rushes out five minutes after I started.

—What are you doing? You're killing the chickens! You're pulling half the skin out! Get outta here! Get out, go, you're fired!

That was my chicken-plucking job that I had for five minutes.

BROOKSIDE MANOR

So I got on the road again and the same guy drives by, he had a route or something.

—What happened?

—I was fired.

—OK, there's a hotel called the Brookside Manor. They need a lifeguard.

—That's me.

I can't even swim. But I'm going to take the job. He takes me there, and the lifeguard job thank god was filled but they needed a children's waiter.

—Do you know how to wait on tables?

—Of course.

So that night I went to the kitchen and put a bunch of dishes on a tray, and I walked back and forth, and I carried the tray balanced with one hand. Now the children's dining room is on the other end of the main dining room which is a football field away, I've gotta walk from the kitchen to the children's dining room and set up the tables for 25 kids – that means a plate, a saucer, a knife, a fork, a spoon, a main dish, a soup dish, god knows what. Then I've gotta go around and take the orders, run back to the kitchen.

So the unwritten rule was they had to give me a dollar per week for each kid, plus I'm getting 20 dollars a month and my room and board, so I'm making 45 dollars a week. I'm making more than my father was, working as a busboy.

Anyway, I waited on those kids. So one of these, little Abie, little Jake, whatever his fucking name was, he used to drink up all the cream. The kid's mother says — Jake, drink the cream. He would sit there, there was always a lot of cream left over. He was a skinny kid, she was fattening him up to go back to the Bronx. For her 15 dollars a week for the kid, she's going to fatten him up. At the end of the week, she's leaving and she gives me 50 cents. I said—No, no, what's this? —It's your tip for the week. —No, no, here. Here's your 50 cents back. —Why? —Because maybe he gets hungry on the trip back, go buy him a couple pieces of candy. I don't need your 50 cents.

She goes to the owner and complains that I insulted her, which in effect I did, I said fuck you, here's your 50 cents back. He comes to me and says — Are you insulting my guests? —You know what that little kid was doing? He was drinking your cream.

We used to collect the cream and bring it back to the kitchen. They wouldn't throw it out. They'd throw it in a big vat and use it again. It was the kind of place where I used to go into the kitchen and sweep up the bread crumbs for the chickens in the back.

The name of the owner was Lander. And he didn't know the English language well enough. He named his first son Phil.

The busboys had to dance at night with the guests. You didn't get to slink off to your room. You had to go onto the dance floor, and dance with the girls there. Otherwise, not enough men around.

They're short of a waiter one night so they made me a waiter. I worked all freaking day, and now I'm working as a waiter at night. There was a Jewish couple, an old couple that used to sing Jewish songs, so I know all the songs, *Mein Shtetle Belz*, etcetera. I know them all because I heard them so many times. The old guy and his wife used to wear white suits, he wore a white suit when he entertained. I'm delivering a load of borscht to him, I spilled it all. I spilled borscht all over his white suit. What a fuckup I was, my god he looked at me. He went to change his clothes.

—Wait, before you go, here's some sour cream.

UP THE RANKS

In 1939, Britain and Germany went to war. The factory calls my father and says — Dave, you still around? —Yeah, I'm still around. —Come back, the factory's opening again.

We were dancing in the fucking aisles, it was great. Pop was making 35 dollars a week now, instead of 14 a week. We could start buying some food again. The war put my father back to work. He didn't retire at 65. He wanted to keep working, and he stayed there until he was 75.

By then, the government knew that we were eventually going to go to war, so they said — Anybody that wants to go to Rowayton, Connecticut, we'll send you to radio school for four or five months, you'll be a third-class radioman. Starting out as a petty officer, you're already up the ranks.

Six of us from Borough Park, five Jews and one Italian, we all went to join the Navy. The one Italian, his name was Dominick Tiscione, he was part of our group, but we couldn't take him to parties with that name, because Jewish mothers wouldn't want an Italian in the group going with their daughters, so we called him Donald Tishman. *Tisch* is table in Yiddish, so he was Donald Tableman.

They all passed the eye test except me, my fucking left eye, shit. 20-100. They said — Step aside.

I sat down in the chair while they were dropping their pants and getting their assholes checked. I'm sitting there dejected. Bad left eye. It's a big open place at the recruiting station. I had a pencil and I had a newspaper. I sat down and I wrote down the eye chart on a piece of newspaper and put it in my pocket. I don't know what the hell I was thinking, but I thought it was a good idea to get a hold of it.

I started to hitchhike up to Canada. I wanted to join the Canadian Air Force, like I'm looking to fuckin' get killed. I'm hitchhiking to

LEON ON HIGH

Canada and a guy picked me up and he said

—How are you on heights?

—I never thought about it.

—There's a job that pays 75 cents an hour, working on construction. It's way up.

—OK.

He took me there. We're building this coal chute. I have a picture of me standing on this goddamn thing with my foreman, 17 years old, I've got a pipe in my jaw. I'm way the hell up, walking on this goddamn two-by-twelve, and it didn't bother me.

When that job ended, I went into Schenectady and I heard that they were hiring boilermaker's helpers. They were building these tremendous boilers that went to ships. They were called Scotch boilers. I thought they were building boilers for Scotland.

I got the job. My job was to be inside the boiler while the outside guys drill holes into the steel, with drills three inches in diameter. It took two men to hold the drill, and they make all the ventilating holes in the steel. I'm hearing this shit, I'm covered in black shit, with other guys in this fuckin' boiler, and some guy's drilling from the outside. You're in a boiler and the sound is reverberating and the drills are happening and the dust and shit is flying.

After six weeks I quit, because I was going to lose my hearing. I might have even lost a little then.

That also paid 75 cents an hour. I was getting as much as my father was getting.

I never did get to Canada, but they would never have taken me anyway because the schmuck that I am, they're not going to take a guy in the Air Force who's fuckin' blind in one eye.

HOLLYWOOD AND VINE

I came back to New York and stayed home awhile.

I couldn't get into the Navy because of my bad eye, but I heard about the National Maritime Union and I read about the Merchant Marine. I went down to join the NMU and get my papers. It cost me 12 dollars. But I didn't ship out of the New York office. There weren't any jobs I could get with brand-new papers.

I went to the Lincoln Tunnel, a car pulled up, he said — Hey kid, where you headed?

—California.

—We're going to Las Vegas, can you drive?

—Yeah, I can drive, I've even got a license.

So I drove one of the cars. They were delivering new cars to California. The way it worked, in California the cars sold for three or four hundred dollars more than they did in New York. They would drive them out to California, and they would wash them down, put brand new tires on them, and they wouldn't run the speedometer. There's a convoy of three or four cars, so I'm in that convoy, and they're all speeding, and I don't like going that fast. I still had a sense of self-preservation. I'm not in a hurry. I went with them as far as Las Vegas, and found another ride to Los Angeles.

I went to Hollywood and Vine, and I got out and there was a place called the Pig and Whistle. I walked inside — I'm looking for work. They said — OK, we'll make you a dishwasher. I said — Fine. I wasn't there long.

I ran into some guy named Murphy and they had a little apartment in one of these garden apartments, and they were looking for a third guy to share the rent. So the other guy was named Boyd, and this guy was named Murphy. I was always impressed with Murphy, because he had a car, he could get under the car and change the oil and all that shit. I couldn't do a thing when it came to mechanics. But this Boyd was a good-looking young man, and he played tennis and used to wear these nice cute shorts, and he had a queer pull up in a convertible, and he used to take Boyd out to play tennis and maybe give him a blowjob. And Boyd lived that way, he used to get money from this queer. Well, Boyd was an extra in movies, and strangely enough, I saw a movie years later and there was a scene with a newsroom and there's old Boyd.

The apartment had a little courtyard in the middle. I used to go out in the courtyard and there was a five-year old child. I used to play with her, throw a ball to her, and she'd throw the ball back to me.

One day she comes out and says:

— I can't play with you anymore.

— Why?

— My mother says I can't play with you because you're Jewish.

—Goodbye.

I'm thinking there's another kid that's gonna grow up to be an anti-Semite.

I got a job in Ralph's Market in the fruit and vegetable department. In those days, there was no checkouts. You wanted a pound of tomatoes, I would put them in the paper bag and staple the bag, weigh it, and write the price with a crayon on the bag. So when they went to check out, they had the bag all stapled together.

So one day the manager comes to me and says — Leon.

This is Los Angeles, 1941.

—Leon, I have to let you go.

—Why? I'm doing my job. I don't fool around. Young, pretty girls come in, buy things, I don't try to make out. I'm very respectful. I'm strictly business. I'm getting 14 dollars a week.

—You're Jewish. Some of our customers are complaining.

—Yeah, I'm Jewish, I don't walk around with my dick out, but what's that got to do with anything? Somebody wants a pound of tomatoes, I give them a pound of tomatoes, I don't converse with them, I don't… whatever.

—Sorry, Leon.

Ralph's Market let me go because I was Jewish.

That's twice. The little girl doesn't play with me, and Ralph's doesn't want me to work there. Can you imagine the anti-Semitism then? I'll be a son of a bitch. That was the first time I was ever exposed to that, because I lived in Borough Park in Brooklyn. There were Jews and there were Italians, but there was no such thing as anti-Semitism among the Jews or the Italians. So what the hell's going on around here?

That was anti-Semitism then, and ever since then.

BUSBOY

I got a job at Earl Carroll's Nightclub. They had a flashing sign outside. The letters would light up to spell **EAT AT THE THEATER**:

```
THEATER
THEATER
THE THEATER
THEATER
```

I started as a busboy. They gave me a jacket. I had my own black pants, but they were too long on me. I'm walking up and down a circular staircase, and I step on my own pants, and a coffee mug on my tray fell down onto a patron. — Oh shit, there goes my job on the first day. They didn't fire me. I went to apologize to the guy, I said — I'm sorry sir. — Alright, kid, get outta here. Long pants, sons of bitches, they don't work on circular staircases.

They promoted me to the help's waiter. There were four to six captains for each section, and about 15 dancing girls, and I would wait on all of them, and each one would give me a dollar a week. I joined the busboy's and waiter's union, so I was also getting 15 dollars a week from the job. I was making 35 dollars a week, which was as much as my father was making at home.

I served these people with steaks, some of them wouldn't even touch the steak. I would go back and I'd eat the steak. Munch it down. I grew up hungry, and here I'm eating leftover steaks, and that was my job.

Earl Carroll, he didn't go for these skinny girls. Every one of them was well endowed, *zaftig* with breasts, my god I never saw such tits and ass in my life. These gorgeous girls, I'm 17 or 18, and I couldn't get near any one of them. You know why? After the show, they'd always walk out and there were these Hollywood people with convertibles, and they would get going with some of these old farts. I recognized some of the guys pulling up, having seen enough movies in my day. These movie people would show up, and these young, gorgeous girls would get in with them. I'm a real schmuck, I can't get near any of them. They're not going to screw around with a busboy. You're a nobody when you're a busboy.

I'd like to say I had one of those Earl Carroll girls, but I'd be lying. In my mind I had them.

BESSIE AND ANNA

Pop had two younger sisters, Bessie and Anna, both very unattractive. They went out to California as single women and they both met Louies.

Annie met Louie Brown who had a gas station, and Louie was a nut. She used to stand there and help pump gas. Then she'd leave early, so when he closed up and came home, supper would be ready. While she's at home making supper, he's accusing her of entertaining men. Unattractive, but a sweet, lovely woman – if you said pass the potatoes, she'd cry. If you say this and that, she'd cry. This Louie was a nutcase, she divorced him.

Bessie married Louie Chudakoff, the eldest son from a multi-millionaire family. The father had a big meat factory and the younger sons all had big businesses. One of them had the exclusive beer distribution for Los Angeles. Big honorary collectors for Israel. Whatever, big time.

Now Louie, he was an epileptic. And they said – Bessie, you marry him, you take care of him, you'll never need to work. As a wedding present, they gave Bessie three homes–a corner home, and the two surrounding it. They lived in this one home and collected rent from the other two. They had money coming in, and they didn't have to buy meat.

Louie had become a very accomplished locksmith. His brothers were rich, and he was the locksmith. He used to wear his brothers' cast-off, custom-made suits, and he'd have keys hanging from all the pockets. I said — Louie, you look like someone taking a bag of cats to the river.

On the roof of his truck, he mounted a ten-foot cutout of a key that said CHUDAKOFF'S KEYS in huge letters. His brothers said — Louie, you gotta stop this. We don't want you showing up in Beverly Hills with our name on the truck. He had to give that up.

They made him a beer salesman. What was a beer salesman? He would sit at home and phone a bar and say — How much beer do you need? He'd write it down and phone in the order. Big job, he got paid well, didn't do a goddamn thing.

He became a *shik-yingel*, an errand boy for all the women in town.

He told me — Me and your aunt, we don't have sex, she doesn't want it.

But he was horny. He wanted me to take him to San Pedro, where the whores are. I said — No, I'm not taking you to San Pedro with the whores. You're going to get a dose of clap and give it to my aunt? You're on your own.

He found a very attractive divorcée who he used to give money to. She needed the money, and he used to bang her. And she had a daughter, who I used to bang. But I couldn't take her to a motel, there was no motels in those days, so he gave me use of his car and I used to drive the car into the garage and drop the doors. I'm in there, and that's what the back seat was for. I'm banging the daughter, he's banging the mother.

Then there was a crippled woman, she was a paraplegic or something. Louie used to take her out for a drive into the country. I saw her once, sitting in a wheelchair in her doorway in Boyle Heights, the Jewish and Mexican part of East Los Angeles.

I said — Louie, she's in a wheelchair, what are you doing with this woman?

He didn't answer me.

WIPER

I got tired of living in Los Angeles, so I hitchhiked up to San Francisco.

I hung out in the NMU shipping hall, and tried to get a job, any kind of job. No jobs came up. The only jobs were on the Matsonia line, but we used to call it the Fruitsonia, because they were all manned by gays, who we called queers in those days, and all the gay guys had better cards than I had. Your cards were timed, and the oldest card had the first bid.

On the wall, there was a sign that said — The Standard Oil Company of California is not unionized. We want to unionize Standard Oil, and the only way we can do that is to get a lot of our members aboard those ships. When there are enough NMU members aboard the tankers, we can strike them.

But the NMU never did unionize Standard Oil. They were too big. They had their own "union."

I went down to Standard Oil and they hired me.

They put me on one of these little ferries out to the Standard Oil docks, about 12 miles out, in Port Richmond.

For two weeks, I was a longshoreman. They give you a place to sleep. While you're waiting for a spot on a ship, they put you to work. Pick up a bag of potatoes, carry them across the gangway into the hold.

A ship came in, and they needed a wiper. I didn't know what the hell a wiper was. They put me aboard as a wiper.

The ship is at the docks, rolling with the waves, listing back and forth. I'm seasick. — Gee, I don't feel too good.

We hadn't even left the dock. Turns out the guy I replaced had been seasick, and the ship had gone to Malaysia and back, and the guy couldn't work at all, he was seasick for five or six weeks. The

LEON, AGE 18

chief engineer nearly shit his head off — We got another one of these fucking guys?

My stomach settled in.

My job was six days a week.

Four days, I was in the engine room cleaning up, wiping oil spills, just walking around with a kerosene rag. Hot and hard work. The chief engineer was always on my ass. —Hey wiper! —Yes sir, yes sir. —Get me a Stillson wrench! Be fast! I run into the tool room. —Hey what's a Stillson wrench? —Here, this is a Stillson wrench. —Get a monkey wrench! —What's a monkey wrench? —Here's a monkey wrench.

Two days a week, I had to wash the crew's clothing, which I was happy doing. We had a commercial washing machine, and I wasn't in the engine room. You'd put your laundry in a mesh basket tagged with your name. When laundry came out, I'd drop it by your door. But in those days, clothing was not colorfast. So I washed all the clothing with some red things, and everybody on this ship had pink underwear. That was a close call. They were ready to throw me over the side.

It's October 1941. We went to Hawaii.

We stopped at every one of the Hawaiian Islands. Hawaii, Kauai, Lanai, Molokai, Niihau, Maui, Oahu. Molokai was the leper colony. They made a movie about Father Damian there, he lived with the lepers for 40 years, then he caught leprosy and died. Anyway, all the islands used to have whorehouses. Mostly, they were Japanese girls, they had Japanese farmers all over the islands. It was two dollars a shot, and I used to visit them all.

Except for Molokai. I skipped the leper colony.

We went back to San Francisco, and then I made a second trip.

I'm in Honolulu. I meet my friend George Soloff, who's in the Navy. We buy a bottle of whiskey and we go to Waikiki Beach. I get drunk, fall asleep on the beach, and wake up 15 minutes before the ship is due to leave. I'm sick, I throw up. I grab a taxi and get to the ship. They're picking up the gangway, but I get aboard. It was seconds that made the difference. The date was December 1st, 1941. Had I missed the ship, I would have been hanging around Pearl Harbor six days later.

We were a day out of San Francisco when we got news that Pearl Harbor was attacked.

RIDING THE RAILS

When World War II started, I knew I was going to go home. I'm not ready to buy a ticket. I had the money I had earned on the tanker, but I don't spend money on transportation. So I started to hitchhike from San Francisco back to New York. I got out to Lake Tahoe, and I got stuck there. I was hitchhiking and there was nobody there. No cars coming, it's late at night. So I did what no Jewish boy has ever done in the history of mankind. I jumped on a freight train. I had seen movies of these kids riding the rails.

I waited until a train came in headed East, and I jumped on. It stops at Sparks, Nevada, and that's where the railroad cops start walking along with their clubs. Any hobo that they catch in a railroad car gets beaten with the club. And arrested. You're stealing railroad services. I look down at the end of the car, near the beginning, the railroad car, out come these cops with long clubs. I jumped off and got lost.

The train takes off. I'm in Sparks, Nevada. It's December. I only have a light jacket on. I figured, well, I've gotta start walking now. And I'm not going to get lost, I'll stay on the track. So I'm walking along, walking along, it's getting late at night. Holy shit, I'm going to freeze to death. It's now below freezing, and I'm walking with this little jacket.

I come across a telegrapher's shack a couple miles down. He sits there with his telegraph and sends messages, what freight train came and so on. I walked in there, half frozen, and he gave me some hot liquid and asked me what the hell I'm doing. I explain how I'm on the way home. He stops the next freight train that came along. I get onto the railroad car in the front car with the engineers, and they drop me off at Salt Lake City.

I went to rent a room in Salt Lake City at three in the morning. I ring the bell of this hotel and out comes this Japanese guy. I said — No Japanese, I'm not sleeping in no fucking hotel with a Japanese in there, with World War II on. So I left and found another place.

I hitchhiked home from Salt Lake City and arrived back at New York in January.

FIREMAN

In January 1942, the government took seven passenger ships, converted them to troop ships, and loaded them up with 20,000 troops to send through the Panama Canal to Australia.

The ANZACs, the Australians and New Zealanders, were in North Africa fighting Rommel, so there was nobody there to defend Australia. The Japanese were threatening to invade the northern port of Darwin.

It took us 42 days to get to Australia. I started out as a wiper. In Panama, a fireman got sick, so they promoted me from wiper to fireman, which is much better. As a fireman, you tend the boilers. You watch the pressure on them. You've got a big periscope, so you can see the smoke coming out of the stack. They don't want smoke. That would tell submarines ten miles away that there's a convoy. So you had to stand there and make sure that the boilers were working, and you had pressures to watch. And they taught me what I had to do, I did my job. It was very hot. I used to stand under one of the ventilators to get some air, it was a son of a bitch, it was hot hot hot.

We arrived in Melbourne, but the water at the dock was not deep enough for big ships, so we were 50 troops into a lifeboat, with an engineer at the tiller, and me, I'm on the bow. We're the first lifeboat to reach the dock in Melbourne, I jumped up, I was the first American to land in Australia in World War II, you can put that down in my obituary.

And I stood up there, and I said — I take this land in the name of Eleanor Roosevelt!

And then we turned 20,000 troops loose on Melbourne, in a country that hadn't seen healthy guys for three years, just kids and old men. We took care of that. Oh my god, what we did to them, the Japanese did to Pearl Harbor.

I walked into a sweet shop. I had a sweet tooth. And there were these six girls sitting behind the counter selling sweets. So I went up and bought some, and I looked at the girls. Put my sweets in a bag. — What are you doing tonight? She says — I'm off at 8 o'clock. She gets off at 8 o'clock, I took her to the local park, and we fucked all night. My god, I can't believe, would you believe it, six times that night? I was almost 20 years old. I might have left a kid or two.

The Japanese weren't going to Darwin after all, they were busy somewhere else, so we left Australia and took the troops to a port called New Caledonia in the South Pacific, and then we came back empty across the Pacific. We made stops for oil and fuel and for food and whatever, at Pago Pago, Samoa and Pape'ete, Tahiti.

I had read Norman Hall's book about all these gorgeous women in Tahiti, these young beauties with grass skirts shaking their asses at the dock. We dock into these ports, all they've got is old ladies with no teeth, or with blackened teeth with whatever they were smoking or chewing on. Betel juice. Old ladies with no teeth? Where the fuck are these gorgeous girls with a shake in the grass? That Norman Hall is full of shit. I'm looking for the young beauties. No young beauties.

I got back, I hung about New York a while, I shipped out, and that's when I started getting torpedoed.

CARIBBEAN SINKINGS

The subs would go after ships at the change of watch, day or night. And they'd always go for the engine room. That disables the ship. If they have to, they finish with their guns rather than waste torpedoes.

I was due in the engine room at eight o'clock. I had to go ten minutes early. The working fireman would explain what was going on, the temperatures and what you had to watch for.

It was so hot in the Caribbean that I even took a shower before I went to work, just to cool off, and I took a shower when I came out of work.

When the torpedo hit at quarter to eight, I had just gotten out of the shower. I flew in the air, lost my towel, lost my clogs. An ammonia tank exploded, and then all the ammonia's in the room, and it's dark, and you've got all this smoke from the torpedo. It smells of cordite explosives from the torpedo and I'm half-blinded, the ammonia affected my eyesight. I couldn't see.

And there was a Negro messman walked by me, and I grabbed the back of his pants, by the belt, and he ushered me out the door and I was right behind him. By myself I wouldn't have been able to find the door.

Once I was out, I'm naked, I rushed into my room and grabbed the bag that I had already packed in advance for such an emergency. In my bag, I had clothing, a bottle of whiskey, and my ten-dollar camera.

I went down to the deck. The ship was starting to sink. They lowered a lifeboat. I went over the side on a rope, still naked. I'm going down hand-over-hand on a knotted rope about 20 feet with the bag over my shoulder. Into the lifeboat, we rode away. I put on a pair of pants in the boat. I was pretty sick, I swallowed some shit, I'm vomiting. Somebody with a first-aid kit bandaged my eye. Somebody opens the whiskey.

Four minutes later, the ship split in the middle and sank. It was gone.

The skipper saw us go down on the lifeboat. He was still there when the ship sank. I don't think he wanted to commit suicide, but as captain, he's going to be the last man off the ship. It's the rule of the sea. You don't abandon ship with crewmembers aboard. That's why you're the captain.

When a torpedo hits the engine room, all the machinery and everything bursts, and hot boiling water goes everywhere, it kills you. Out of 42 members of the crew, we lost about 20. And I would have been one of them if it had been just a few minutes later.

Now we're waiting to get rescued. The next morning we take pictures with my camera. I wrap the film in electrical tape and put it in my pocket.

We were picked up the next day by another ship. I asked a crew member — What's your cargo? He says — We're carrying ammunition.

We were torpedoed that night.

I jumped into the water, about a 50-to-60-foot jump. We were told when you jumped, to cross your arms and hold on to your lifejacket with your hands. It was a cork jacket, and if you hit the water, the cork could pop up, hit you in the chin and knock you out, so you held onto the jacket. You also crossed your legs because there may be some dunnage in the water and you don't want to fall on anything that would impede your manhood.

I'm floating in the water, and about 200 feet away, this German U-Boat comes up. Holy shit, I'm looking at this thing come out of the water, with the Nazi emblem on it, and they picked up one of the crew members, Archie Gibbs, his name was. They grabbed him and took him prisoner for three days. I'm thinking, if they had picked me up, a Jewish guy on a German U-Boat? Mentally, I already had an Italian name in mind. If they come and grab me, I'm a classmate of mine in public school, Tony Speduto.

TRINIDAD

We were rescued by a third ship, which took us to Trinidad.

I was in the hospital for about a month. While I was at the hospital, I started taking inventory. The German U-boats sank all 18 ships in the convoy, every one. It was a death ride. A historian of German U-Boats found out the names of the two subs that sank me. Both of them were also sunk by American destroyers. I don't know if that's satisfaction, but it's wartime and that's it.

What pissed me off was that in the Navy, I would have got a Purple Heart. In the Merchant Marine, what happened after the ship was torpedoed? They stopped pay. Why? — Fuck you, you're not working anymore, why should we pay you? So I spent a month in the hospital, I'm surprised they didn't charge me for the hospital bill. I'm a fucking war veteran that's wounded.

After I got better, I was still there for a couple weeks. So there's this bridge in Trinidad over the river, where all the lepers and disabled, diseased, and blind people used to sit and beg. They all had baskets so people walking by would have to throw a penny or a nickel in. So for a gag, I went and joined the lepers and beggars, sitting there, crossed my legs with a big basket, I'm sitting here and the guys are walking by — Hey, there's Leon sitting on the bridge!

And then they flew us back to New York. They wanted to put us back on a ship, but I said—I'm not getting back on a ship. But a cadet from Kings Point who had been sunk twice with us, he and an engineer got drunk the night before, and they missed the airplane, so they were sent back by ship. Would you believe it? That ship was torpedoed. So the cadet got back to Kings Point, three times a torpedo survivor. That's how I know about Kings Point. Here's a young man, he's a junior officer, and he told me about the Academy.

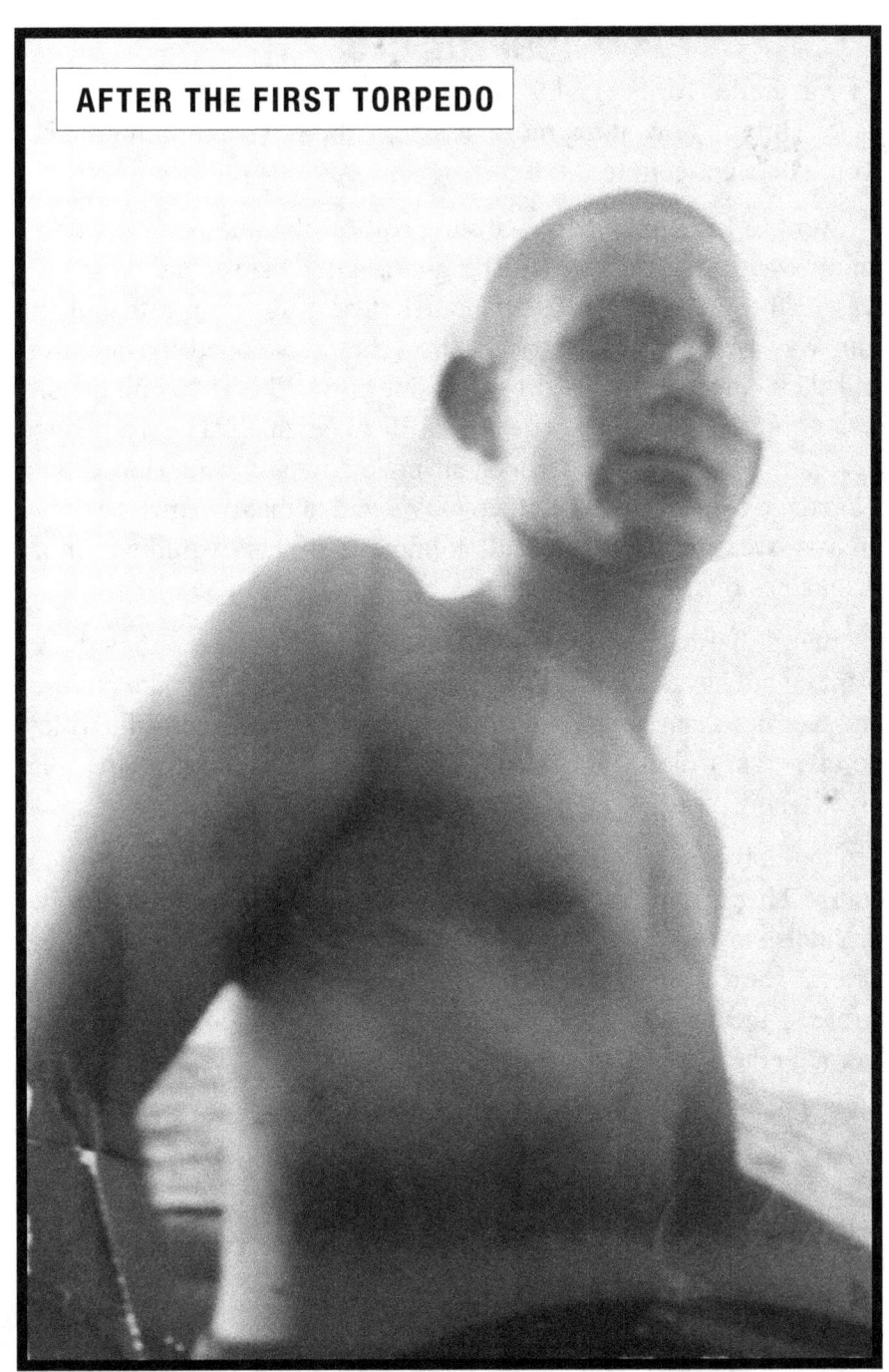

AFTER THE FIRST TORPEDO

TORPEDO CLUB

I was in the Torpedo Club. They gave me a medal to wear on my jacket. I don't have it anymore, it's gone the way of all things. That would be a collectible.

I went to LIFE magazine with my roll of film and said — I don't know whether these will still be good. After the second sinking, I was in the water about a half hour before I got on a raft, but the film was wrapped in electrical tape. They developed the pictures, and they came out with sort of a faint glow, like 1880s pictures. I was going to be on the cover of LIFE magazine, "The Torpedoed Seaman," standing on a lifeboat, stripped down wearing shorts, with a bandage over my eye. But then they decided that two girls with big breasts, wearing what they call Johnny Jeep hats, would sell more magazines than Leon Schneider.

A ten-dollar camera, it was called a Kodak Vigilante. They didn't want you to have cameras on the ship, because cameras take pictures and Germans can get a hold of the pictures. It was one of the rules, no cameras. I didn't give a shit. Nobody gave me shit for it. Who gives a shit for rules?

A ten-dollar camera, that got me 300 dollars. That was a fortune. Of course, I became a local hero in Borough Park. My mother used to write in Yiddish to *The Daily Forward*, letters to the editor called "The Bintel Brief." They always published her letters. When I got torpedoed, she wrote to them, and it was in the *Daily Forward*, a Jewish boy from Borough Park in LIFE magazine.

I decided — no more shit, I want to become an officer. I'm as smart as my brothers are.

I wanted to go to Kings Point Merchant Marine Academy.

TESTS

Paddy Haggerty and Leo Hecht were crew members with me. I invited them to our house in Brooklyn.

Leo Hecht was a real fighter, a tough Jewish guy, a sailor, and he took a fancy to my sister. But I told my sister — No, don't go near this guy. My sister listened to me.

Leo Hecht, he had fought in the Spanish-American War in the Lincoln Brigade. And he and Paddy Haggerty were ardent Communists. They invited me to come down to one of their meetings, and the way they enticed me — There are girls there and there's a lot of free love, you know what I mean? You can have all the women you want.

I was just smart enough not to go. It's a good thing because when I went out to go to Kings Point to get my commission in the Navy, they checked up on you. My name would have been appeared. All the names that went to these Communist "parties" were being taken down by the FBI. My name would have been on it as a Communist. — Why would you go to a Communist meeting unless you were a Communist?

I took the physical to get into Kings Point. I was OK in every regard except my eye. I had the eye chart memorized, which I had written down in 1939. In those days, they had different eye charts on a spindle. I show up, and by luck, there's my eye chart.

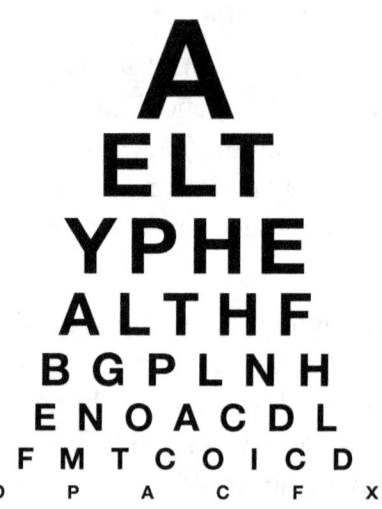

I said I went to the Stuyvesant High School, and they never questioned it. They gave us some tests to make sure we were up to the scholastic level to be an officer, and fortunately, I had enough of a background that I was able to pass. My parents had bought the *Book of Knowledge*, we had all these books and you paid 25 cents a week to buy them. I used to read that, so I had enough savvy.

But when it comes to navigation, you need trigonometry, I used to go home weekends, and Henry would teach me. The sine of this and that – and suddenly, boom, I accumulated it. The brain is good. I just wasn't educated.

I'm still a schmuck. I was competing with guys who were college graduates, 21-year-olds with degrees. I'm the only one who never went to fucking high school.

If you failed an exam, they gave you a rewrite. An if you failed the rewrite you were out. You couldn't fail the same exam twice. That included navigation, cargo handling, signaling, ship's architecture, any of the 15 subjects. One guy, Tiny Tim we called him, he was on all the committees and all the other goddamn things, but he neglected his schoolwork. They didn't give a shit that he was this and that. Out he went.

I didn't join shit.

Oh, and then they would notify the Army. At Kings Point, you had a deferment. We were all healthy young men, allegedly. The minute you failed, the draft board was notified, and you were called and you were put into the goddamn Army. Three months of training and then you're in the fucking D-Day invasion, getting shot at by Germans. I didn't need that shit.

I wouldn't have been drafted into the Army because I would have failed the eye test. If they wanted me in the Army, fuck that, I didn't want to be in the fucking Army. At least the Navy, I would go for. But to be a fucking soldier in the trench, not for me.

I cheated to get into the war, but I could have stayed out of the war altogether.

RULES OF THE ROAD

I got to Kings Point, I worked like a sonofabitch.

When you take the test to be an officer, you're allowed a grade of 70 percent on most things, but with *The Rules of the Road*, you had to be 100 percent. That involved what, when, how you turn, how you do things, how you navigate the ship.

I took *The Rules of the Road* and I memorized the freaking book, and when I sat to take that test, I ran the memorization through my mind and I answered it perfectly. So I'm blessed with a good ability to memorize.

Listen to this, I still remember it.

> *Be it enacted by the Senate and the House of Representatives of the United States of America and Congress assembled, that the following regulations for the prevention of collision at sea shall be followed with all public and private vessels of the United States, on the high seas, and in all waters connected therewith. A seagoing vessel will carry (a) on or above the foremast, or if a vessel without a foremast, in the fore part of the vessel, a bright white light shined twenty points of the compass, and so fixed at the shoulder light or right ahead, and two points of aft and beam, on either side, and so fixed to show at a distance of five miles.*

Can you imagine, I had to memorize all that shit?

I was regarded pretty well because my LIFE magazine article was posted up on the bulletin board, and I had three medals – a medal for each ship that I was sunk on, and one for being in the hospital, the Merchant Marine equivalent of the Purple Heart.

For a while, I got up a half hour early. I played a record of a bugler playing *Reveille* and woke everyone up — Let go your cocks and grab your socks! — and then gave them exercises over the loudspeaker.

LEON, CADET

But you know what? I needed that extra half hour, I quit the job.

The officers would come in and examine your room wearing white gloves. They would climb up on the bunk, and run their hand up on top, and if there was dust on that glove, you were restricted for the weekend. No pass. We used to get away on Saturdays and Sundays.

They also allowed Jewish guys out on Friday nights to go to the synagogue. You know me, I'm not a synagogue-goer, but I went anyway, just to get some different air and see some women. The only women at Kings Point were two old ladies that worked in the shop selling Coca-Cola and candy.

On the weekends, I'd ride home. On the Long Island Railroad, I'm studying *The Rules of the Road*. I get home, and Henry is giving me lessons in trigonometry. I'm sitting on the toilet seat, I'm reading *The Rules of the Road*.

After the first six months, we spent the next six months at sea as a cadet. We went to Casablanca. As a cadet, I'd stand watch with an officer on the bridge.

There was this Polish son of a bitch, Shturkin, he was a cadet with me for the six months at sea. He was a fucking anti-Semite, he would always just throw this bullshit at me. We get back for the final six months at the Academy. One day, I'm walking along on the campus at Kings Point, and there was this prick in civilian clothes. —Hey, whatcha doing? —Geez, I failed, I flunked out. —Oh, that's too bad.

I knew that the son of a bitch, he'd be in the Army in a week, and that was before D-Day. —Aha, I hope you're right in D-Day, get your head shot fucking off.

That takes care of guys that shit around with me.

OFFICER

I graduated from Kings Point in 1944. Mind you, a high school dropout, a bum stealing money off counters and stealing fruit from food stands.

Sonia and my mother came out to Great Neck to watch me get my diploma.

Pop wouldn't take the day off to come and see his bum son wearing a white uniform, getting a diploma, becoming an officer. He was getting 75 cents an hour, so six bucks a day. I should have told him — Pa, if you don't show up, I'm never going to talk to you again. Take the fucking day off. Get on the goddamn Long Island Railroad for fifty cents and get up to Great Neck and see your bum son get a fucking diploma.

My two genius brothers, mathematics awards, science and everything, both of them were 3rd class radarman. And me, the fucking high school dropout, I'm an officer.

ELEANOR

I met Eleanor Roosevelt. She came to Kings Point to make a speech and I took a picture of her. I gave that to the Academy, and my photograph of her is on the wall now.

Eleanor Roosevelt and I practically hung out together.

LEON, ARNOLD, HENRY

THE BLITZ

I graduated at the bottom third of the class but I got through. And there happened to be one subject I was good at, shipping economics.

Commander Bull calls me into his office. He says — We see your shipping economics is good. Would you like to work for the War Shipping Administration? We'll send you to England, and you can represent us and work with the British Ministry of War Transport.

I said — Great, I love that.

I've been at sea, I've been sunk twice, and the third time might be the last time. So I'm glad to be on land.

They sent me to Washington, D.C. for two weeks of orientation. While I'm in Washington, the Chamber of Commerce calls me to say — We want you to come up and speak at a War Bond rally about your torpedoings.

—I'm not a speaker.

—Just go and talk about what happened to you.

There was Admiral Land sitting up there on the rostrum with me, I'm now with Admirals. There are three thousand people sitting there. I got up and told a joke — You know the definition of driving in Washington? Capitol punishment. And then they couldn't stop me. You know me. Once I got rolling, I talk and talk, and they gave me big applause, and then they shipped me out to London.

We land in London, and what do you think, the fucking Germans are dropping bombs all over. What the hell am I getting into? I'm supposed to get to an air raid shelter, and then I'm lying in the road covering my privates with my helmet. Bombs are dropping all over.

Then I'm walking along, it's dark, it's blacked out, you can't see a foot in front of you. I'm walking with my two hands in front of me, so I don't run into anything. I touch something soft and yielding in the murk. It was a breast.

—Oh excuse me, madam.

And out of the murk she says — Oh, are you a Yank?

—Yeah, I'm an American.

—How would you like a bit of a do?

Now, I'm from Brooklyn, I understand English.

—A bit of a do, how much do you charge?

—Oh, three and six and Bob's your uncle.

Who the hell's Bob? Three and six, how much is that? Seventy-five cents. After the rocket bombs, I need a little, you know, relaxation.

—OK, let's go to your room.

—Oh, this is wartime mate, I ain't got the room.

—Ah, forget about it, next trip.

I'm a brand-new ensign. I'm not going to lie in the road like some freaking animal getting laid.

—Oh no, no, Yank, don't go away. You see the building over there?

—The building is gone.

—Oh, but the steps are still there. I'll get on the second step, and we'll be eye to eye, and we'll do it standing up.

—That's great, I like that, yeah, what do you call that?

—Oh, we call that a knee-trembler.

The fuckin' English, they're funny.

So she gets up on the second step, picks up her dress, and I wiggle around.

—What now?

—Bump your ass, Yank, bump your bleedin' ass.

—I'm bumping my bleedin' ass, but why is your head bobbing up and down?

—Oh blimey, I have me scarf caught.

I dropped me load, I wipe me tallywhacker on her scarf, she walked off whistling "God Save the Queen," and I said — I take this land in the name of Eleanor Roosevelt!

I'm in London one day and already I'm bombed by the Germans and get a knee-trembler? This is going to be a great war.

I took my helmet and gas mask, and off I went, tally-ho.

WAR SHIPPING ADMINISTRATION

As ships would dock, I would go aboard and ask them — Do you need any crew members? And do you need any food?

We had a big storage warehouse, and we had things in there which the Britons hadn't seen in years. Like oranges. Oh my goodness, you could get laid for an orange. You can't believe what two oranges would get you. I had the keys to the kingdom.

I met a Jewish girl. She said — Come on, I want you to meet my parents. So we went down to the Underground, and we walked along, stepped gingerly along people sleeping on the platforms. I stepped on one guy, and he's on top of this woman, and the woman looked up and said — Thank you! We came up to her parents, and she said — I want you to meet Leon, an American Jewish boy from Brooklyn, New York. Like I said, the keys to the kingdom.

I had a big truck, and a GI would drive me from the warehouse to the ship, where we'd unload whatever they needed. And if they needed any crew members, we'd see that they'd get replacements. I didn't always have the driver, so picture this, I'd be driving a 30-foot diesel truck on the wrong side of the street, shifting with the wrong hand, and guess what? You can't put any lights on, because a light would be seen from above, so I'm driving in the dark. I have a helper in the passenger seat. I say:

—We must be getting close.

—Why do you say that?

—Because we're hitting more people.

Then they sent me to Cardiff, Wales. When I rented a room there, the landlady says — I have two young children here, so I don't want you coming back here with any women visitors. —OK, I'll take the room.

I met a girl there. I can't take her to my room. There was a railroad that ran from Cardiff, Wales to a place called Pontypridd, Glamorganshire. I would take this girl and a fathom of rope onto the train. There were two doors in each passenger compartment, out to the corridors on either side. We would jump into one of the compartments, and I'd throw a figure eight around the door handle and run the piece of rope across to the other door, so the door was virtually locked. It was a 30-minute ride up to Pontypridd, Glamorganshire. We had the cabin to ourselves, and I did my dirty work.

I think her name was Barbara. I have a picture of what she looks like in my mind. I remember she had a great dimple on her cheek.

VICTORY IN EUROPE

The job ended but the war was still on. Had I stayed, I could have been an official with the steamship companies. The guys that stayed all became top operators and managers. But I wanted to go back to sea.

I was in Southampton, England, and got on a Liberty ship called the *S.S. John Brown*. I only had a third mate's license, but they made me acting second mate, which is the navigator.

We are at sea when the Germans surrendered. We got the RCA cable, and I asked the radioman to make me a copy, which I donated to the Merchant Marine Academy.

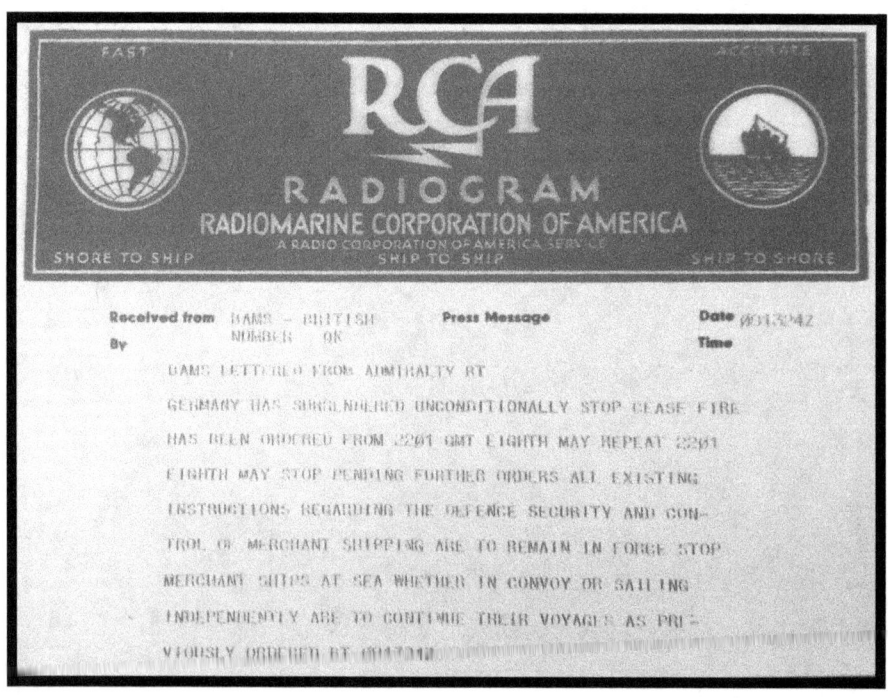

Our ship went up the Scheldt Estuary into Antwerp. It was the second ship of the first convoy to get into Europe after World War II ended.

Then we went to Germany. I'm at the dock, and I'm watching these Germans. I had pictured the Germans marching with Hitler, these thousands of troops, all in order. These were raggedy-ass kids and old men. This is what's left of the German army. I stood there, I'm a Jewish officer standing, looking at these guys. I saw Bremen and Bremerhaven, bombed to fucking shit. If you picture hell, this was hell. I felt good inside to be a Jewish survivor. I'm looking at these Germans, these were not the big fucking Nazis that I pictured or saw in newsreels, these were fucking raggedy-ass people picking up scraps of food.

You could get laid for a pair of silk stockings, the German girls hadn't seen those for years.

But you know what I noticed in Germany? A lot of educated, bilingual German girls shacked up with Black soldiers. These were uneducated farmhands out of the mountains of South Carolina or Georgia who didn't get past grade school. Highly-educated German girls would pay them thousands of dollars to get the hell out of Germany as a war bride. The girls had the money, they were working during the war. If they had stayed, they were looking at food shortages, and all the grown men were either dead or conscripted. In America, they could get food, nylons, and a divorce.

I picked up a Rolleiflex camera for a carton of cigarettes. We're docked somewhere and I go ashore. I come back, the third mate is on duty and he had the key to all the rooms. He comes up to me and says
— Leon, I needed some alcohol. I needed a bottle and I didn't have any money, so I went into your room and I took your camera.

Now if I had gone into my room and found it missing, I immediately would have investigated. I would ask — How could my camera walk out of my room, when you're the mate on duty, the only man who has the keys?

—You took my camera? And sold it because you needed whisky? I'll tell you what. It's a 300-dollar camera. I want you to go to the captain immediately and get me my 300 dollars, or else I go to him and report you. It's the end of your license. You realize that you'll never sail again as an officer.

So he went to the captain, got 300 dollars, and gave it to me. Not a bad deal for a carton of cigarettes.

About a year later, I'm at the union hall looking to ship out, and who comes up but the third mate.

—Hey Leon, you son of a bitch, 300 dollars? I was able to buy that same camera for a couple cartons of cigarettes. Give me my 300 dollars back.

—Get the fuck outta here before I knock you on your ass. You come to my room and steal my fucking camera, it's a 300-dollar camera.

—I got the same camera. I'll give you the camera back.

—I don't want it. I've got your 300 dollars.

PUTTING UP THE RITZ

I'm the third mate on a freighter in Le Havre, France. The war had just ended, and there were still no passenger planes flying back yet. We're heading back to the States, and as a freighter, we can take 12 passengers with us. More than that, we'd need to bring a doctor on board. We don't have passenger accommodations, since every room was taken by the crew. Instead, we emptied the stern, moved the cans of kerosene and oil somewhere else, and put in plywood bunk beds with skinny mattresses for the 12 passengers, and a big five-gallon drum with holes poked in it for a shower, and they have to bathe with salt water.

I look at the passenger list and one of the names on the list is someone named Ritz. I went up to him to introduce myself. —Mr. Ritz, are you in any way connected with the Ritz Hotel in Paris?

He says — I'm one of the owners of the Ritz.

—Sir, you're a participant in one of the finest hotels in the world and you're sleeping on plywood with a three-inch mattress? No, no. Look, I'm on the 8 to 12 watch, so I'm on the bridge between 8 p.m. to midnight and 8 a.m. to noon. When I'm out, you're welcome to come to my room, read my books and magazines, take a private shower, listen to my music, and enjoy yourself in the luxury of my cabin, you're welcome to it.

—Mr. Schneider, I'll be eternally grateful, and if you're ever in Paris, my hotel is yours.

I'm such a schmuck, I never took him up on it. Well, it was a very nice thing that I did and it cost me nothing. Of course, I didn't leave any watches or jewelry around. You never know with these fucking rich people.

RELIEF AND REHABILITATION

We landed on a dock in Naples, Italy, and we've got ten thousand tons of food for the Italians, UN supplies from UNRRA [United Nations Relief and Rehabilitation Administration].

The captain had to leave to go to Rome. He had medicine for some very highly-ranked people, penicillin or something, and every time they shipped it, it was stolen. At this point, they gave it to the captain and said — Put this in your safe, and when you get to Naples you will get on a train and deliver it by hand to the individuals whom we nominate to receive this medicine.

So the captain left. —OK, Schneider, you're in charge.

I was the first officer, but after my eight-to-five shift, I was off duty. I would go ashore.

This Italian gangway watchman spoke English. He said — Leon, what do you do when you go ashore? I said — I look for the nearest whorehouse.

I don't drink like other guys. I look for a whorehouse to get laid, and then I go and have a good meal.

He says — Look, I know a nice woman, you don't have to go to the whorehouse. This woman is supporting a child. She's not a whore, but I'll fix you up with her. Give her the money that you'd give to the whores.

I said — That sounds good. So I go to visit this woman in her apartment, and she's living there with her mother. I want to take her out to dinner, she wants to bring her mother, fine, I take them both out to dinner. We walk by a store, they want me to buy them gifts, fine, I buy them gifts. I take them to the theater and we see a show. We go back to the apartment and I'm with this girl all night. She convinces me to stay overnight, which wasn't hard to do, so I stay until morning.

I get back to work at eight o' clock. The second mate had been on duty. He said — The ship has been robbed. I say — What do you mean the ship has been robbed?

A boat had pulled alongside and they emptied the galley. They emptied the stores. We started with stores for 90 days' supply, and we had only been out 10 or 15 days. All the stores were emptied into the boat, leaving us naked.

I said to the second mate — Didn't you see anyone? How could you look the other way when there's a boat alongside unloading *our* cargo?

He was in on it. He got paid to look the other way. Oh, they were trying to bribe me on the ship to sell the cargo. I said — Get out, I don't do that kinda shit. This stuff gets delivered.

I don't sell government property to screw around, I'm not that dishonest. Sure, I was selling black market cigarettes, but I'm not cheating anybody, I'm just making a little spending money.

The captain comes back from Rome.

—How's everything?

—Captain, we have to resupply the ship.

—What do you mean? We left with 90 days' supply.

—We were robbed.

—You were robbed?

He accused me of being in on it.

—Why weren't you aboard?

—Look captain, I put in my eight hours, and I leave the ship with a responsible officer in charge, and I go ashore. I don't put in a day's work and then sleep on the ship. We're in dock. I go ashore to a hotel. I want to have a life of my own for part of the day.

He accused me of negligence for not staying aboard. The Army came aboard, investigated, all that shit. We had to restock the ship. It cost probably $100,000 to put food into the ship again.

The captain kept blaming me. —You should have been aboard.

Later I found out that that second mate started a trucking company with the money that he got from looking the other way, and he became a big trucking man. Son of a bitch, I didn't wish him well but it didn't do me any good.

Once was enough, I'm through with buying gifts for the nice woman and her mother, so I went to the local whorehouse. I go inside and who do you think the whores are? The nice woman and her mother. The mother is the madam and the nice woman is one of the working girls. —You're a fucking whore and I'm taking you out to dinner and buying you gifts?

When we were out together, people were looking at me funny. They know who the whores are in town.

The guy at the gangway fixed me up with a fucking whore, who kept me all night so I wouldn't interfere with the theft. I went back to the gangway man, I said — You son of a bitch, I oughta throw you into the fucking ocean. You fixed me up with a nice girl, and she turns out to be a fucking whore. You really fixed me up good, eh? A nice girl living at home with her mother.

—Ooh, I didn't know.

That was my trip to Naples. I brought home a lot of Borsalino hats.

JAPAN

Japan had *geisha* girls. They weren't whores, they were just companions. They would just sit and pass the wine glasses, and they'd work on the fish and cut the steaks for you.

I saw the devastation we had done to Japan. I didn't see Hiroshima or Nagasaki, but I saw Yokohama. My God, what we did to those Japanese. I said to myself — you fuck with the United States, boy, we had to build the ships, we had to build the planes, we had to train the soldiers, we sent them to different countries all over the fucking world, and we kicked your ass. But you know what? We're not the kind of ruler that takes over and enslaves the country. We gave them food, we brought them money so they could get back on their feet.

I also remember bringing *weekies*, a set of seven underpants of different colors, each labeled with a different day of the week, Monday, Tuesday, Wednesday. For a set of *weekies*, you could get laid for two weeks.

WAR BRIDE

We were leaving France on a freighter with a half-a-dozen passengers. We had a party in my room, and I invited the passengers. I had my tape recorder. And they all came to my room and I played my tape recorder and I taped everybody's comments and then we played it back and everybody had a great time.

One of the girls aboard the freighter was a war bride. She was French, and American soldiers in France married French girls. They screwed the French girls, too, but some of them married French girls. She had gone back to France to visit her family, and now she was coming back to her husband on the freighter. She and I hit it off, so she used to sneak into my room at night. In the morning, there were people walking around, and so she would climb out the porthole onto the deck and walk back to her room.

I hadn't met my wife then, so I was not cheating on her. I was cheating on my hand.

But she was cheating on her husband.

I might have knocked her up, who knows.

ROSITA

I first went to Argentina in 1947. We docked the ship in Uruguay and I went ashore that night. I crossed the Rio de La Plata to Buenos Aires.

I went to a nightclub and I'm sitting there. They would have girls sit with the sailors and make the sailors buy them drinks with the promise of sex. But at four in the morning, when the nightclub closed, the girls were greeted outside by their big boyfriends, and the cops were there, so the girls ignored the sailors. —Wait a minute, I've been buying fucking champagne for you all night. This so-called champagne was *gornisht*, it was seltzer water, but you were paying champagne prices with the promise that they were going to take you to bed. All the horny sailors are laying out all this money.

Anyway, I'm sitting at this table and this dancer Rosita sits next to me, and we start talking. She doesn't speak English, I didn't speak Spanish. But she's speaking to me, and I said — Do you know German? And she spoke to me in German, and I spoke back. And she said — That isn't German, that's Yiddish you're speaking. I said —How do you know? And she says — I'm Jewish. —Rosita? —No, my name is Rosie. Rosie Asher.

So we started communicating, and we had a romance while the ship was there, and then I decided I wanted to come back.

GRRRRAMMI

I went to a steamship company run by the Greeks. They were sending a ship to Narvik, Norway, north of the Arctic Circle, to load iron ore. The ship was then going to Uruguay to be turned over to the Uruguayans.

So I went up there and I said — Look, I'm a navigator, you don't have to fly me back, I want to stay there. They said — Great. They're saving the cost of one fare. They hired me as second officer, the navigator. My pay was a third of what Americans were paid, but I didn't care. I'm getting free passage, I'm working my way down there.

I go down to the Argentine consul and I have to submit papers and get documents from the New York Police Department that I'm not an escaping convict. They look up my fingerprints, I'm clean, so I get a passport for Argentina, I'm free and clear.

This was an old Greek coal-burning freighter, with guys in the hold shoveling coal into the boilers, the hairy beast down in the engine room. The only coal-burner I've ever been on.

We're still in port, and the toilet seat which all the officers used was all shitted up, so I got the steward to order a brand-new toilet seat. The ship leaves port. We're out at sea. I go back aft expecting to see the new toilet seat. Where is it? Oh, the captain's got it in his personal quarters. The captain liked it so much, he put it in his toilet. I'm still stuck with the dirty toilet seat. Fuck this guy, I'm not going to shit on a thing that's already got turds on it, so I disconnected the toilet seat and walked out on deck with it. Usually there's a third mate, second mate, and first mate, and the captain. On this ship, there was no third mate. The captain stood the 8-to-12 watch that would have been the third mate's job, so they're saving one officer by using the captain as a watch-stander. The captain is on the bridge, and I walk out on deck, and he's looking down on me, and I've got the toilet seat in my hands, and I flip it over the side. A fucking act of defiance. He didn't say anything, never said anything.

On American ships, a waiter would take your order from a menu, and there was a choice of meat and fish and whatever, they always fed us well. On Greek ships, there's no menu. They put a big pot of food in the middle of the table and it starts at the captain at the head of the table, and the chief engineer, and they pass it around to the lower ranks, and you put your spoon in there and take a spoon of some shit, and put it on your plate, and by the time it gets to me, I'm scraping the bottom of this fucking thing. That's Greek-style dining on freighters. I survived.

On my watch, I have a man steering and I have to give him orders. Now, he doesn't know English, I don't know Greek. I got the Greek word for steady as you go. Straight. —*Grrrrammi!* So in the daytime, he's at the wheel, I'm looking out, I want to make a move, there's a buoy, there's another ship, I wave my right hand or left hand which obviously he followed by putting the wheel to the right or left, and then when I got it lined up to where I wanted on the compass — *Grrrrammi!* He'd have to repeat the order. —*Grrrrammi!* Steady as you go. At night, he couldn't see me because there's no lights in the wheelhouse, your eyes have to be accustomed to the dark. So I'd get behind him, and if I wanted him to turn right, I'd tug him on the right sleeve and he'd put the wheel to the right. When it lined up —*Grrrrammi!* —*Grrrrammi!*

I *Grrrrammi*'d all the way to South America.

We get into port, and they drop anchor. The ship had to stay at anchor for a couple weeks until it found a place on the dock. Now the captain, he's not standing at watch anymore, so it's just me and the first mate, 12 hours on, 12 hours off. OK, that's my job. I start to put in 12 hours on, 12 hours off. At the end of my first week, I put in for my overtime. On American ships it was $1.50 an hour. The

Greeks only paid 35 cents. But even 35 cents is money, so I put in for four hours overtime in excess of the eight hours, that's what the law is.

The first mate says — Hey Schneider, this is a Greek ship, they don't pay overtime. —You mean I'm working 12 hours a day for dick? —That's the way it is. —Goodbye. They wanted me to stand extra watches with no overtime? I said —Fuck you. There was a lifeboat that would take the crew members ashore and then take them back when their watches were ready. I got into a lifeboat and said —Fuck you, I'm not even staying on the ship. I go onto shore, and now the captain's stuck, he's gotta stand my watch. I'm ashore in Montevideo and they're not paying off for another ten days. I checked myself into the local whorehouse and I spend the next ten days in the whorehouse.

On payday, the crew came ashore and the captain came with money. I showed up, and he smiled. He knew they were trying to shit me around. — Hiya captain, how you doin', how's your watch-standing? —Yeah, OK, Schneider. He paid me off.

INVENTION

I took the night boat from Montevideo and crossed the Rio de la Plata to Buenos Aires. I had a passport and a visa. I went to the hotel. I looked up Rosie. She came up to my room.

Soon, three policemen come up with a big, sturdy-looking German, Herr Schnapp. They saw there's an American checking in at the hotel, they looked at my passport, they're checking up on me, they want to see who the hell I am. So they come up to my room, these three Argentine mobsters and Herr Schnapp, who's a German who worked with the police. I say to her in Yiddish — *zug gornisht*. Say nothing.

That was just Argentina under Peron, it was like fucking Germany. They came up to see who the hell I was. We're not doing anything, we're all dressed, we're not in bed. She's just sitting there, a visitor. — Who are you? — I'm a visitor. — OK.

Herr Schnapp, of course he knew what I said to her, *zug gornisht*. So after that he came up to me and I had to befriend him because he was hanging on the ropes. I used to take him out and buy him a meal. He joined me and we got dinner together and he'd regale me with stories of whatever happened to him in Germany.

He was a stout German, you couldn't choke him. He had a neck about size 20. He said — Choke me, choke me. I put my hands around his neck and he tightened his face so that the neck muscles all stood out, you couldn't choke the guy. So he came to me one day, he says — Leon, I have an invention, but in order to get it patented, I want you to take my invention back to Washington and patent it or get a patent lawyer. But I need the money to make the model, in order to patent something, you have to have a working model.

—Well, what is it?

—It's a device for your car. If you're sitting upright in your seat, and your ass makes contact with my invention, you're able to start the car, and should you faint while driving or have a heart attack and fall over, it disconnects and the car stops.

—That's a great invention, great.

—I need money for that.

—Nah, not my kind of work.

The son of a bitch tried to hustle me. It was a fucking hustle, the fucking maniac he says he wants the money to make a model, I said — No, no, Herr Schnapp, I'm not buying it.

That was Herr Schnapp. That was my introduction to Buenos Aires.

Rosie moved into the hotel with me. I have a picture of her. Great-looking girl, blonde, good figure.

I had real serious plans with Rosie. This was a very good-looking girl who danced professionally. I was even planning on taking her back to the States, and I was serious. Now one day a guy comes up to me and says —Do you know that Rosie is married? —Huh?!? —Rosie is married and her husband is a piano player in one of the clubs here in town.

What the fuck. She was married to the piano player. I went and visited him. I went to the nightclub and said — You know, I'm Leon Schneider. He said — I know about you, you're living with my wife, we're still married. —I just wanted you to know I didn't know she was married, I wouldn't have bothered.

I say to Rosie — What's going on with you? I'm taking you back to the States to introduce you to my family, and marry you, and now I found you're married?

—Uh, I didn't want to tell you.

—You didn't want to tell me? When were you going to tell me? When I proposed marriage, and you said yeah, you'll marry me?

You don't care that you've already got a husband?

—Let me tell you the reason I'm not living with him. In 1939, right before the Holocaust started, a lot of Jews knew enough to get the hell out of Germany. It cost them money. They had to bribe German officials, but those German officials took the bribes and whatever jewelry or artwork they had and let them get the hell out. I went to my husband, we had savings, I said I want to take my savings and bribe some German through some intermediary that handled that, to get my parents out of Germany. He refused to give up all his life savings and mine, together, and the inevitable thing happened. Both my parents were taken to the Holocaust and died. At that point, I moved out and refused to have anything more to do with him. We didn't get a formal divorce because in Argentina, it's such a Catholic country, you can't get a divorce, you have to know the Pope personally, so we let it stay at that. That's the reason.

—Well, that's not good enough for me. Our relationship is over. If you had told me this before, I could understand it, and maybe go through some legal means to dump this guy, but you kept it a secret, so we're over. We're finished. I said — Fuck off, you didn't tell me you were married, that's the end of you, goodbye.

REFUGEE

While I was in Buenos Aires, I met this Jewish girl Evelyn. I still have a picture of her. She wrote in Spanish on the back of the picture —I'll never forget you Leon, I love and blah blah.

And I befriended a German-Jewish refugee in Argentina. He made his living by going around peddling, a lot of them did that. He used to go out to the outskirts of Argentina and sell pots and pans on credit. He'd make the rounds, he'd get these Argentinian housewives pots and pans, and write it down in his book, and then he'd come and collect a peso now and then. He survived. I used to buy meals for him too, and he said — How you doin' with Evelyn, are you screwing her? I said — Look, I don't talk about that, I go with girls, I don't talk about whether I'm screwing them or not. I wasn't, actually. I'm going with this kind woman, she's a very reputable woman. Her father had a big trucking business. And she spoke enough English that we could get along very nicely.

After I left, he started going with her. When I came back a long time later and I asked about it, it turns out he married her. They went to Brazil and they started a very successful business. He became a big-time operator in clothing, a manufacturer of dresses and coats and shit. And he married this girl. I said — Well, it's nice to hear that story.

PESOS

I had been making money on the black market. Argentine pesos were four to a dollar, legally, but if you had dollars, you could get six pesos on the *black* dollar, so I used to go aboard ships with a lot of pesos. When you draw money from the captain, he gives you the legal rate. You say — I want a hundred dollars. And he gives you 400 pesos. I went up to the crew members and said — Don't take from the captain, I'll give you six for a dollar, not four. So whatever dollars they had, they gave me. I went ashore and changed their dollars into pesos again, and I would get a little bonus, I would make like ten percent, so if I changed two thousand dollars on a ship that afternoon, I made two hundred dollars. I'm making good money, and Rosie kept telling me — I need this, I need that. So I kept giving her money. Who cares, we're living together, you need money, here's money. I got it. The money was coming out of my ears. I was *americano muy rico*. I'd take ten people to dinner and pick up the tab. Nobody paid. I was a big-shot rich American, they don't know that I'm making it black market. What happens? The money system changed, I wasn't able to get in and out of the ports that well, and then suddenly, all the money that I was making, it disappeared, it filtered down. I was spending big time, I'm now broke, so I decided I've gotta leave Buenos Aires.

I was shacked up with some other dancer, who danced with her brother. Her brother was gay. We all lived in the same room. We hung a sheet to divide the bed. I was fucking his sister on one side of the sheet and he was on the other side.

I was broke. I was so broke, I had to pawn my class ring and my sextant, because my money disappeared so fast. I'm waiting to get on a ship.

So I went to Rosie. We're not communicating anymore, but I went to her and I said — Look, I gave you a lot of money when I had it. Now I'd like some of it back. I need it. I'm broke.

She refused.

—No.

—Rosie, don't make me do what I have to do.

—What do you have to do?

I said — Do you remember the first night, when we arrived? In my hotel room?

I said — Now, if you force me, I could go back to Herr Schnapp, who I befriended, he's always on me for a free meal.

I said — I'm going to have to tell him you're a prostitute. You know what? A prostitute in Argentina, a Jewish girl, a prostitute, you'll be sent back to Germany tomorrow.

I said — Look, you put me in no position, my sextant and my ring are in hock.

She wouldn't see me anymore she was so fucking mad at me, so she sent her friend with the money who came up to me and gave me my money.

That I needed.

That I wanted back.

Not all of it, of course.

Enough to bail my sextant and my ring out.

The friend says — Leon, would you have done that?

I said — Don't ask. We didn't come to that. But she was holding out on me and I needed it. Come on, I was good to her, and …

—Alright, Leon, goodbye.

That was the end of Rosie Asher.

POOR ALFREDO

I was staying in Uruguay, waiting for some kind of a ship, and for a time I was hospitalized in Montevideo. They put me in a hospital bed next to a man named Alfredo. He came from a highly wealthy Uruguayan-English family. He was a very athletic type. He rode horses, and he had his own racecar.

We're lying in beds next to each other, and his girlfriend used to visit him. This was one absolutely stunning girlfriend, and she wanted to be alone with him, and he wanted to be alone with her, but I'm there, I'm not leaving. I'm looking at her, this is a gorgeous girl. So he hits the call button on the bed, and the nurse comes in, and he motions toward me. She says — Leon, please, come out, you have to come out, they have to be alone. So I got out.

He told me about how it's so important when a high-class Uruguayan-slash-Englishman marries, the girl has got to be a virgin. A lot of girls were not virgins, but there was a doctor specializing in making virgins out of non-virgins by sewing up their vaginas. When a guy married one of these girls, he's poking into her and his poor dick is hitting these stitches inside, and there's a little blood showing up there, aha! This is a true virgin. That's how non-virgins became virgins in Uruguay.

Months went by. I left Uruguay.

I came back to Uruguay six months later when I was on a ship, and I called, I wanted to say hello to Alfredo, see how he's doing. His mother answers the phone and I said in whatever Spanish I knew — *Yo deseo hablar con Alfredo.*

So she said — *Alfredo está en el cielo.* Alfredo is in heaven? *Está muerto.*

— *Lamento*, I'm sorry.

I hung up. Then I made inquiries. I found out that he was making practice runs in his racecar, speeding along at 120 or 140 miles an hour and he didn't quite make the turn and he was decapitated. Poor Alfredo, my friend in the next bed, who had this absolutely gorgeous girl, god damn, we're talking top Hollywood beauty. I tried to remember her phone number.

Poor Alfredo.

DECKHAND

I finally got a ship. I said — Where you going? They said — We're going back to San Francisco. So I signed on as a deck maintenance man. I figured I'd work as a deckhand for two weeks.

It turns out there's a strike on the West Coast. The ship gets a letter that says — Do not come back, they're on strike here, so we're redirecting you to the Philippine Islands, where you'll take a load of rice and you'll bring it to China or some other goddamn place. I said — Holy shit, I signed on to be a deckhand for two weeks. I ended up a deckhand, a deck maintenance man, just above an able seaman, for four or five months.

My mistake was letting the boson know that I'm an officer with a chief mate's license working as a deckhand who he could tell what to do. He broke my balls. I'm now a fucking deckhand for four or five months, and all the shitty jobs were given to me. If someone had to climb up under a winch and scrape away the rust on their hands and knees? — Hey, Schneider! The halyards on the mast, one of the ropes broke. The only way to retrieve it is to climb up the mast, step by step, and then shimmy out on your ass straddling the cross-tree. Now the ship is out at sea and it's going from left to right, port to starboard, and I'm on this fucking thing 150 feet in the air. And I'm crawling out inch by inch until I retrieve it and replace the broken line and then crawl on my ass backwards to the ladder. Oh, of course he got me to do it, no one else. And you can't turn a job down.

I worked with a little guy who was a fantastic mechanic, and he was given an order to splice wire. There's nobody on ships today who can splice wire. I learned how, with this guy, he taught me, and we get to splicing wire. We took eight-inch rope and made eyes out of them. We had a 50-foot roll of wire, and we had to cut our own and then start making splices. I can't even explain it, it's pretty complicated. It's a real sailor's technique. Today, when a ship needs rope with an eye in it, they order it and it comes with an eye in it.

The Philippine Islands were nice, except Manila. Manila had all these crazy little cops running around shooting anything they can. I'm in a bar in Manila and suddenly these cops start shooting. What the fuck. Even though I came from Brooklyn, I'm not accustomed to gunshots. I dropped down on the floor with everybody else. And Manila had what they called the Billy Boys. These were young men walking around, they're gay, and a lot of them had their breasts made, doctors do that shit. You're walking around in Manila and these Billy Boys come up to you. — Get the fuck outta here.

The other islands I liked, and I went all over the islands there. Nice, gentle people. There were four or five of us, we rented bicycles on one of the islands. We're riding along and we came along a bunch of girls running out to meet us. All these girls jumped on the handlebars and we pedaled to the local swimming hole, and we all jumped into the water, naked of course, and I'm fiddling in the water and there's this one girl, and we did it underwater. Well, I mean some of it was underwater. So I might have left a kid in the Philippines, I don't know.

I went back there with the Korean War, the Vietnam War. I've been all over the islands.

Anyway, for four or five months, I worked as a deckhand. We finally got back to San Francisco and I got paid off.

EXODUS

The Jewish underground came to me in 1947. Israel wasn't a country yet. I think they knew I was Jewish because when I was at Kings Point, I went to synagogue on Friday nights to get a break from the Academy.

They said — We need you as an officer. We have a lot of Zionist kids, but they can't navigate, they can only be messboys. We need men who are qualified to run ships. We need officers and we want to recruit you.

I said — Well, uh, OK, do you pay anything?

They said — No, we don't have any money.

I said — Well, I take care of my parents. I help them out. I pay their rent and their utilities when I'm working, and if you can't pay me, what do I do then?

They said — We'll take care of it, how much is it?

I said — It's 80 dollars a month.

They said — We'll take care of that, Leon.

At the time, I was a second mate studying for my chief mate's license.

They said — You have to be available when we call you.

I said — I'm home studying, and it's a six-month program of study, and the exam takes 10 days.

They called me after the ninth day of my exams.

They said — Leon, leave tonight for Baltimore.

I said — I'm all yours, I'm going to work for nothing, but I can't leave tonight. I have one more day at my exam. If I leave now before the exam is over, I have to start all over. I've progressed to the ninth day. I have one more day, then I get my license, and then I can go tomorrow.

They said — You have to go tonight.

I said — I cannot go tonight.

They said — Sorry, Leon, we have to get somebody tonight. Goodbye.

They got another guy to go as second mate.

It was the *S.S. Exodus*, trying to bring Jewish refugees to Palestine. The British Navy attacked the ship in the Mediterranean, and the second mate resisted the British and was killed, and that made the British look bad, and well, you know the rest. I was one day away from being part of Jewish history. I'm sorry I missed it. I would have liked to have been part of the fiber of the whole country starting out.

Not that I would have resisted the British. If I'm there instead, maybe there's no Israel.

At any rate, they said — Leon, you didn't make the ship, but we'd like you to come to Israel and teach navigation. We want to start a maritime and you could teach navigation. I said — No, no, I'm a seagoing man, I'm not a shoregoing man. I don't know Hebrew. They said — No, no, don't worry about that. I said — I forgot my Hebrew. They said — Everybody here speaks English. I said — No, I'm going to stay at sea.

That was my second offer, to be an instructor for the Israeli maritime.

I stayed out at sea.

ISRAEL

I was all for the State of Israel. It was 1948, they're starting a country, and of course I'm aware of the Holocaust and all the terrible things that have happened, and they're starting out a new country.

Our next-door neighbors in Borough Park, we were all very friendly, they had a lot of children. Well, they all packed up and went to Israel. That was the one family that I knew who went.

I've never gone there. I can't stand those Orthodox guys that run around and want to run the country, the real super-Orthodox ones. I'm Jewish, culinary-style. All them people annoy me, they're fanatics, they walk around wearing garbs from the 17th-century Polish shtetl that they lived in and they want to enforce all that crap. I like bacon. I like ham. I like *poak chops*.

I'm not happy with what's going on at the moment. They're not treating the Palestinians well, they keep building and building. They're doing to the Palestinians what the Germans did to them, which is not nice. I'm not sympathetic with them anymore. I don't say boycott, but come on, give these Palestinians a break, they're living for thirty years on the outskirts, being directed by these Israelis who became very tough and very smart and very exploitative.

Palestinians are still human beings, these are children being born thirty years after all this shit happens, they don't deserve to be treated that way. These people deserve to live, the way the Jews deserve to live in 1948.

I'm one of those Jews saying — Slacken up a bit. Stop building in their towns. Let them live. Let them take their land back.

IRELAND

Not long after Queen Elizabeth got married, I was in Ireland visiting my sister and her husband, who was the American vice-consul in Belfast.

They had a friend who had a big linen factory there. Before, he had a big conglomerate in Europe, but then the Nazis took it over so he moved to France. Then they took over France, and he ended up in Belfast. He kept opening factories. And he gave me twelve napkins, big square napkins, the same ones that were given to Queen Elizabeth when she got married the year before.

I met a Rolls Royce dealer who took a liking to me. He said — Leon why don't you stay? I'll give you a job. He was offering good pay for Belfast, but I was making three times more as a ship's officer.

YUGOSLAVIA

When the ship docks, I have to report to the U.S. Embassy and check in. Sailors didn't have to have passports, so I'd go to the embassy and present the documents of the ship, so that all the crew members are allowed to be in the country without a passport.

The ship was going to be there for a while. Someone at the embassy introduced me to a ballet dancer, a beauty. We started keeping company.

At the time, the Yugoslavs were pissed off at Americans for giving Trieste to Italy. Any American they saw in Yugoslavia, they would beat up. I started wearing a black raincoat and a beret. Nobody associated Americans with berets. Once, we were walking down the street and there were a bunch of Yugoslavs at the bottom of the street. If they knew I'm an American, I'm in trouble. She starts speaking to me very loudly in Yugoslav, and me with the beret, we walk right by, so I didn't get beat up.

We drove out to a resort called Opatija, any Yugoslav would know it, and we spent the night there. That night, someone slashed all four of our tires.

She was one of the leading ballerinas in the ballet, but they gave her nothing. In New York, a top ballerina would have fur coats and Chanel dresses, but in her room, she just had a couple pieces of clothing. I looked around and said — They don't treat you very well. She had to work for the state. She had to dance all week at the ballet, and occasionally on weekends, she had to go out fifty miles away and perform for the troops. And she got nothing.

I thought about getting her the hell out, renting a sailboat and going somewhere, but she had no papers, no passport, so I just had to write it off.

Had I been able to get her the hell out, I would have had a Yugoslav wife and you would be speaking Spanish.

KOREA

I'm the first officer on an extended Victory ship, 800 feet long, and we're taking locomotives to Korea, and guess where the locomotives came from? The Schenectady Locomotive Works. The two guys accompanying these railroad cars come aboard the ship and they're talking to me about how we're going to secure all that shit and I say — Hey fellas, you know something? I worked in that boiler factory. And now I'm the first officer.

I landed in Korea in 1950. On a dock down below was my brother in a War Correspondent's uniform, and he was standing on the dock waiting for me. I brought my brother a present, a 14-inch Hebrew National salami, so my brother had a party and they're eating Hebrew National salami which they thought was fantastic. I brought other things too, like a big ham and this and that. I brought a lot of food that they wouldn't have over there, because I knew he'd be there, but I didn't know where or when.

I had my 28th birthday in Pusan, Korea, and my brother threw me a party. There were 23 courses in the meal, due to my rank as the first officer of the ship. I asked — If the President of the United States showed up, how many courses? They said — It would be 125 different courses. There were 20 men and 10 *kisaeng* girls sitting with us, and they would cut the food and pour the wine and light your cigars.

I was presented with two vases which we still have today. They're about 12 inches high, made from bomb shells from a cannon, painted and enameled. Maybe your mother will put my ashes in one of them.

CONVENT

I stayed at the Palace Hotel in San Moritz. I checked in for two weeks, but I was running low on money and there was a nice hotel down the street. So I checked out of the Palace Hotel into this less expensive one, and I'm sitting there at the second-rate hotel, and I see this girl sitting across, eating alone. So I tell the waiter — Send over a drink, compliments of the man here.

I send over a drink, she looks my way and nods, and I raise my glass. Then I go talk to her, she's telling me her story.

She was raised in a convent, a nunnery in Austria, but then she grew up to be an interpreter in Italy. She spoke about five languages. I invite her to my room, she came in and we started having a little activity. Then I told her — Look, I come back here every six weeks. I was on a Mediterranean run. She said — I'll meet you, I can take time off. So she started to meet me in all these ports. This was great, a highly-educated woman, every time we docked, I didn't have to go to the local whorehouse, there was this lovely woman meeting me.

She told me the story of why she was in Switzerland. She went with this Italian guy for 10 years, and he said — I can't marry you because I have to take care of my mother and brother and whatever, and I can't take responsibility for a family. She finds out the guy's immensely wealthy and could have taken care of a whole army. Anyway, she had a nervous breakdown and that's why she went to Switzerland. She was about 40 years old.

And she started asking me questions about my family. I told her — Smart brothers and sisters, all very attractive, top scholars. I didn't pay any attention to those questions at the time.

This went on for about six months. Finally, one time she didn't show up. I wrote to her and said — Are you OK, is there something wrong? I never heard from her. I wrote back — Hey, I'm sorry, did

I do anything to offend you? The last time we parted, we seemed to be OK.

There was one time she couldn't find me. My ship was going to Livorno, which we called Leghorn. She was going by the Italian name, so she didn't know where to meet me. She went to the consulate and they straightened her out. She found me that time.

And then it occurred to me. She wanted me to make her pregnant. I know, I know it, I have the strongest feeling, my instincts said — She just wanted me to make her pregnant.

I never heard from her again. I must have a sixty-something-year-old heirloom floating around Italy.

LAW SCHOOL

I had been at sea for a number of years, and I was getting tired of it. I was about 34 years old. So I applied to the New York Law School. I thought I'd get a license and be an admiralty lawyer. I already had my master's license. So they said — Sorry, Kings Point is not pre-law, you know how to navigate and tie knots but it has nothing to do with law, you have to go to pre-law for a couple years and then you can go to regular law school. I said — No.

Four years later, I'm thinking — You know what? I should have done it anyway, because four years later I was still at sea. And that's how I spent the rest of my life.

GI BILL

Both of my brothers served at the end of World War II. Both of them were given GI Bill of Rights, and they never heard a shot. Me, I've been torpedoed and shot at and pissed at and everything else, I couldn't get GI Bill of Rights because I was in the Merchant Marine.

They gave both brothers the GI Bill, and some woman that lived in Kansas who was a telegrapher, she was given the GI Bill.

But the Merchant Marine? —Fuck you. Your ship was sunk? — We stop your pay. I was in the hospital, I didn't get a Purple Heart, I got shit. They stopped my pay when I was sunk. That's what I got. The Navy, they were sunk, they get the GI Bill of Rights, everybody gets the GI Bill of Rights. The Merchant Marine? —Fuck you, step aside.

Until the next war, they don't need us. But when they need us?

—Hey, we need you, come back, come back.

—Fuck you.

We never got it. We tried. We went to court. It went up before Congress and some fucking Congress said — eh why should we give them any money. It would have been such a pittance. It would have been a penny.

—Fuck you, you're a civilian.

They couldn't give anything to the Merchant Marine, who died in bigger percentage numbers than the fighting Marines. If you had a son, I'd say — Do not put him in the Merchant Marine.

We had guys in the Merchant Marine who were 4-F. They wanted to serve in the Army but they were turned down, so they joined the Merchant Marine. The physical for joining the Merchant Marine during World War II was very thorough. Two doctors examined you. One looked up your ass, the other down your throat. If they could see each other, you were rejected!

We had a messman on the ship who had some kind of severe physical disability when he was born, with one arm bent in close to his body, and he limped. He put the broom under his armpit and limped around sweeping up. Here's this guy with a handicap, one arm practically useless, out at sea.

And then you have John Wayne, he plays generals and big-time admirals. Big fucking hero, he stayed home. How did they make him a hero? He's a fucking draft dodger, like this goddamn president we have. Bone spurs.

SUEZ CANAL

I've never been to Israel. You know why? When I was on ships, we would transit the Suez Canal to go from the Mediterranean to the Indian Ocean. We don't load fuel and water to go around the world, we stop at various ports. We stop at Gibraltar, we stop at Saudi Arabia, we stop anywhere we can get fuel and water, we do it in leaps and bounds.

The Arabs said — We cannot stop you from transiting because you're an American ship. However, we're going to look in your logbooks, and if you've been to Israel, we will not give you food or water. You will transit the canal but you cannot get any courtesy.

The ship can't run without fuel or water, so the ships I would run always avoided Israel for that very reason.

So I'm the first officer on a ship going through the Suez Canal. The Egyptians come aboard and they want to see the crew list. I said:

—Why?

—We want to know if there are any Jews on the ship.

—Look, we're all American, we sign on people, we don't ask people their nationality, or their origins, or whatever. They're all American.

—But they could be Jewish. They could be Israelis, or they could be closet Hebrews, they could be Zionists in their heads. They could drop a bomb in the water, they could block the passage of ships, they could disrupt the whole transit system, they could destroy the Suez Canal. We have to protect the Suez Canal.

—If there were any Jewish seamen, what would you do?

—We would put them in their cabin, and an armed guard would stand outside their room, and they would not be allowed to leave the cabin until you transited the Suez Canal. They'd be served food inside and accompanied to the toilet.

They're going to put me in a cabin and lock me in with a guard outside the door? No way. Nobody's locking any of our crew members up with an Arab standing by with a gun.

— No, no, there's no Jews on the ship.

There happened to be three. Now, I never ran around with a Star of David on my neck yelling — I'm a Jew! I'm a Jew! But this is the only time I said — No, I'm not Jewish.

My name's the first on the list.

—Schneider?

—German.

The second guy was Rudinoff, an ordinary seaman, a lousy one at that.

—Rudinoff?

—He's Russian.

Steinberg was the messman. You know I got a weird sense of humor.

—What is he?

—He's Mexican.

Now we're transiting the Suez Canal, and time is money with this ship. It costs thousands of dollars to keep a ship running. The faster you can get there, unload, and get back, the more money the company's making.

The pilot in the Suez Canal comes up and says to me — I have to drop anchor.

—Why?

—I have stomach distress, and I have to go to the bathroom, it's serious.

—No, no, do not, drop no anchors here. We cannot wait an hour, that's an hour that'll cost the company twenty-five hundred dollars. I'll take over.

—You'll do it?

—Yes, goodbye, I take responsibility.

—You're on your own.

I navigated the Suez Canal for 30 minutes while he took a crap. Steady as you go. Back and forth, there are buoys and I've got a chart and I know how to navigate. I know starboard, port, red lights, green lights. I see a camel, steady up on the camel's ass. The pilot comes back, everything's fine. So I'm a part-time Suez Canal navigator.

I was in Egypt and said to one of the Egyptians:

— It's very hot here.

I got out a ChapStick and rubbed it on my lips.

—What's that?

—It's an oil product, we take the oil that comes out of the ground, we take it home, we make it into a product and we put it on our lips.

—We don't have such sophistication here. This is Egypt.

—What do you do?

He goes up to a camel, puts his finger in the camel's ass and rotates his finger. He takes his finger out and rubs it on his lips.

—Does that keep your lips from getting chapped?

—No, it just keeps you from licking them.

End of story.

I tried Camels for years. I still prefer my wife.

ANKA

Paul Anka was 17, and he made a cruise on our ship. I didn't know who Paul Anka was, I didn't follow these fucking young singers. But his agent arranged for teenage girls to come to every dock where the ship docked, and scream — Where's Paul? We want Paul!

I dock at this place, I'm at the gangway, my job then was to see that everything is orderly going off the gangway, there's no shoving or pushing. The people walk down, it has to be orderly.

And a bunch of kids come up yelling – Where's Paul Anka? Where's Paul Anka?

So I yell back to them — Anka's Away!

Could only use that joke once.

OCEAN AVENUE

I had an apartment at 1250 Ocean Avenue in Brooklyn. I used to rent it out to a friend, just to cover the rent and the utilities when I was gone.

I rented it once to a girlfriend of a friend of mine. I come back, I get a phone bill for a lot of money, she had been calling a friend of hers way the hell out.

Then I looked around, and I went mad.

The girlfriend of my friend, she used my beautiful linen napkins to clean the dirty stove. I went crazy. I charged up to where she was working. She worked for a minister.

I said — You wiped the stove with my linen napkins? That was practically the same thing that Queen Elizabeth had? And furthermore, you owe me a lot of money for the phone calls which you made.

—I don't have the money.

I said — You'd better get it, you'd better get it. Otherwise I'm going to tell your employer, the minister that you work for, that you're a goddamn whore.

She was screwing my friend, a lawyer that used to come in. She screwed the lawyer on weekends. Some other guy, she screwed him during the week, he couldn't get away on weekends.

I said — I'm going to tell the minister that you're a goddamn whore.

She said — No, no. She took care of it.

But I could never forgive her for wiping the stove with my napkins.

FLATBUSH

When I'm home, I used to hang out at this restaurant on Beverly Road, everybody used to gather there at night, right in Flatbush. All the neighborhood people, one woman there with her daughter, a lot of guys, I knew everybody there, I would go there every night and schmooze around.

One of the guys there, he was a cashier at a railroad ticket office. He said — Do you like to gamble? I said — Yeah, I'm a crap shooter. He said — I know a moving crap game, and this is all run by the mafia. It's a floating crap game, I can take you. I said — Yeah.

The way it would work, you'd go to a place, the outside said Limousine Service, you sit in a room, six or eight of us on the bench. A car would come in and pick us up, and take us to the floating game, which was in a different place every time. The first time they took me there, they patted me down to make sure I wasn't carrying a gun. These were all tough mafia guys. And for some reason they thought I was a lawyer, I don't know why, I didn't say yes or no. So I showed up at these floating games with 500 dollars at a time. When I'd lose the 500, the shylock there would loan me 500 but I had to pay him back the next day, 25-dollar vig. And you'd better show up with the 500 the next day.

There was one time I was down to six dollars. I bet wrong, six to five that it doesn't make it, so it didn't make it, I got 11. I started shooting, I went on a twenty-five-minute roll. I hit every number on the dice, and one little mafia guy saying — Keep shootin', kid, you're doing good. This was a guy who lost thirty-five thousand dollars the previous night. And he shows up the next night with a load of bills again. Where the hell do these guys – anyway, I don't question where they got the money, they don't question mine. I ran it up to four thousand dollars. I bet the last twelve hundred on the come-out, and I lost. I counted my money. I had twenty-eight hundred dollars. So I went up to the guy at the door, and I gave him fifty dollars, and I said — Don't let anyone out for thirty minutes. I'll get my car and get the hell out of here. You see, a mafia man is not going to be afraid, he'll walk out and you're not going to screw with him. But I'm just a passerby with twenty-eight hundred dollars, someone could overtake me and say — OK kid, give me your money or else. So I get home and that's the last time I ever went back.

I had a girlfriend at the time whose teeth needed a little work. I took her to my dentist and said — Do whatever you have to do, fix her teeth and I'll pay for it. That's what I did with my gambling money, fixing people's teeth.

PASSINGS

My brother Arnold died young. He had rheumatic fever as a kid. He was about 45 when he died. I went and saw his body in the hospital. He had an apartment in New York and a farm in Pennsylvania. There was my poor brother, he was still warm. You know why? He had all these machines pumping into him. And you know how they tell if you're dying? They put a thermometer up your ass, and if the thermometer keeps dropping, they know that you're dying. That's the last indignity. You're lying there, being resuscitated by machines, and you've got a thermometer up your ass. And after that, they use it as an oral thermometer.

In 1966, I was on a run to Puerto Rico and back. A radioman came up to me when I was on watch with a telegram, and he said — I have bad news for you. And I read it. My father had died.

He was hit by a car while crossing the street. He was walking to get his rolls and daily newspaper in the morning. This guy was speeding, hit my father and hit four other cars, and then finally stopped. And then when it went to court, they brought him up and he says — The old man was walking against the light.

My father's eyes weren't that good at his age, he was 87, but he would never walk against the light. So the driver got away with it. Had I been home at the time, I think I would have killed the son of a bitch.

THE OLD CONVINCER

That *Love Boat* was such a bunch of bullshit. You don't dance with the passengers, you don't go to their cabins.

If you want to fuck 'em, wait till port.

I'm on this one ship, I was the best cruise director on the bridge. People would come onto the bridge for a two-hour lecture on what's happening, and there was nobody on the fucking oceans who gave a better tour than I did. They wouldn't want to leave. They'd show up at 10 o'clock and by 12 my watch is over and they want to stay. Two of the girls stayed. Next thing you know they said — Give us your number. They called, they showed up in my apartment, and then they came in. I was ready to get into bed with both of them and I said — Girls, how old are you?

—Seventeen —Seventeen-and-a-half.

—Thank you very much, I know my arithmetic, it doesn't work that way. So nothing happened.

I give this lecture and there were about 20 people on the bridge. I let the young kids take the wheel, they think they're steering the ship, of course it's disengaged, it's on automatic pilot. The kids are having a great time, the adults enjoy the show.

I get a phone call saying — One of the women that attended your lecture on the bridge would like to go out with you when you hit the port. Her name is Miss Tishman.

I don't recall her, there were 20 people there. They gave me a room number. I called and said — Hi, this is Mr. Schneider from the bridge tour. Miss Tishman? — Yes? —We're hitting a port soon, it's a beautiful beach, shall we go? She said — Oh, I don't like the sun. I said — Look, there are umbrellas, we can rent an umbrella and you can cover yourself with sunscreen. It's a beautiful place to go. — Okay.

I said — How will I recognize you?

She said — I'll be wearing a pink costume.

On shore, I can fuck her. On board, I can't do that.

So I get to the gangway. She said she'll be waiting at the bottom of the gangway, and I'll be off watch at noon, so I'll be down there at 12:15 after I change into a bathing suit.

There's this old lady standing at the bottom in a pink costume. These guys fucked me up, they played a big trick on me. —Miss Tishman wants to meet you. They knew that she was an old broad, so I walked down and she's wearing this pink costume and I said — Miss Tishman? —Yes. Mr. Schneider? —Come along.

I couldn't say — Fuck off lady, I'm 30 years old, I'm not interested in 75-year-old women. So we go to the beach and everybody was in on the big joke, all the crew members are sitting around, they're having a great joke — Hey, Schneider's going after the old broads now. And there's Miss Tishman and me under a big umbrella.

I took her back to the ship. —Thank you, Mr. Schneider, for a lovely afternoon.

I said — My pleasure, my dear.

But I said to myself — No seconds, lady.

I look back at it, maybe I should have tried to slip her the old convincer. I found out she was divorced from a multimillionaire. She would have been a wealthy woman. If I pursued her, I'm marrying into wealth.

Have I ever screwed older women? All the time! Listen, my dick has no memory and no vision. A stiff dick has no fucking conscience.

A stiff dick will fuck a snake if you hold its head open.

THAT'S IT

I was the navigator on a big passenger liner, the *S.S. Argentina*, and we docked in Bermuda. I went out looking for women. I'm at a club and I ask this woman to dance, and we dance, and then she says — Now, dance with my friend. —What, her? She looks 16. —No, she's 23.

That was your mother. They were on the wrong cruise, a British ship with newlyweds and senior citizens. No young people interested in two girls.

I'm 42 years old, and she was 23. I took her number, and then I saw her in New York. And then I continued sailing. I run out to Vietnam, came back, went back to Vietnam, meanwhile we're corresponding all this time. I went to South America and came back. I saw her for a brief period every time I came home.

Finally, after about three years, I realized — I don't think this girl's going to wait too long.

I decided — Well, that's it.

I came back, then we got married, and you know the rest.

Three children, two mortgages.

TAMARA

SEVENTEEN'S YOUR POINT

In 1975, an advertising agency in Kingston was willing to pay Tamara $25 per day to be a full-time designer. With three kids at home, Tamara couldn't afford to take the job.

Tamara received an unexpected call from *Seventeen*. The art director had just been fired. They needed somebody to step in for two weeks to finish the issue.

Tamara went to New York and finished the issue in one week. The managing editor suggested that she apply for the art director job, and she did. Tamara met the new editor, Midge Richardson, and the interview continued for three hours. ("It was like meeting an old friend that I hadn't met yet.") Tamara was invited to stay for a subsequent staff meeting, and she knew almost everyone there. She got the job.

For over six months, Tamara commuted. She took the two-hour bus ride to New York first thing on Monday mornings. During the week, she stayed in the Bronx with an aunt and uncle, which shortened her commute to just an hour on the subway each way. She returned to Kingston on Friday evenings.

In 1977, Leon and Tamara sold the Kingston house for $60,000 and bought one for the same price in Montclair, New Jersey, a commuter-friendly town just 17 miles from Manhattan.

After several years with *Seventeen*, Tamara became the first woman art director in the hundred-year history of *Ladies' Home Journal*.

Leon stayed home with the kids.

EXTRA

In the mid-1980s, a photographer friend of Tamara took headshot photos of Leon. Leon began modeling in print advertisements. One photo was turned into a television commercial, and on that basis, Leon received a waiver to join the Screen Actors Guild in 1991.

I've appeared in over 30 movies as a background extra. If you're an extra, you get $150 per day, and if you speak one word, you're "featured" and you get $850.

In *Law and Order*, I was a judge, banging my gavel and yelling — There will be order in my courtroom or I'll empty this courtroom immediately!

The director comes over and says:

—Just mouth the words, Mr. Schneider.

—If I mouth the words, does that mean I'm no longer getting the 800 dollars?

—That's correct.

Fine, you fucked me. So I mouthed the words. — These motherfuckers are cheating me out of my goddamn money and fuck 'em all.

Anybody who can read lips would know what I said.

And then it happened again. I'm a doorman dressed in a uniform at Macy's in New York. My job was to stand there and hold an umbrella. Susan Sarandon comes out, I call for a taxi, and escort her to the car. For that one word — *Taxi!* I'm going to be a featured actor.

Then the director comes up and says — Leon, just mouth the words.

So I never got a speaking role.

Once, I was a stand-in for Eli Wallach. I talked to him and told him about my background and all my experiences. Then I sent him a letter with some photos, and he wrote back and said — Leon, with all the things you've done, I should be making a story about you.

I was an extra in *The Sopranos* at that Ding Dong bar, whatever they called it, and the announcer says — And now we've got these three famous dancers that will come out and entertain you, the Three Manhattans.

Three big-titted girls come out, they're dancing to the music, and I yell out — Three Manhattans and not a cherry among them!

I got thrown off the set.

The highlight of my career was a commercial with MCI, listening to a kid playing the violin. I ended up getting tens of thousands for that one. Plus, they sent me a check for 800 dollars, a holding fee, and they said — You cannot work for any other telecommunications company while you've got this commercial. I was so excited I came in my pants, I just got 800 dollars for not working.

This is a great country. I'm glad my father came here.

PENSIONER

Twenty-three years as an officer, and I never had a collision.

I got my unlimited Master's License in 1956. I'm qualified to be the captain on any size ship in the world, on any ocean.

I put in for my pension and I got it in 1969, so I've been getting my Masters, Mates & Pilots pension for 50 years. Unfortunately, it's not indexed for cost of living like a government pension. I was getting five thousand dollars a year in 1969, and it's still five thousand a year. When I first got it, it was money.

The pension stops when I die. Every year I have to write them a letter, notarized, that I'm still alive.

I'm 97. The secret to longevity? Keep breathing.

I have sex almost every day. Almost Monday, almost Tuesday…

ABOUT THE AUTHOR

Ivan Schneider works as a ghostwriter and copywriter for large global consulting firms, technology companies, and high-tech startups. He collaborates on custom publications and other creative endeavors with his mother, **Tamara Schneider**, who provides art direction, design, and illustration.

Ivan attended Carnegie Mellon as an undergraduate and worked as a database programmer before earning an MBA from Vanderbilt and completing a full-year course studying the Japanese language at Cornell. Then, he worked for five years at CMP Media as an editor for a trade publication in financial technology.

In 2012, he earned his Master of Liberal Arts from Harvard Extension School, concentrating in Foreign Literature and Culture with a thesis on the talking-dog short stories of Cervantes, Hoffmann, Gogol, Kafka, and Bulgakov. In 2017, his article "The Search for Dog in Cervantes" was published in the Animal Narratology special issue of *Humanities*, a peer-reviewed, open-access journal. He has presented his research at the Harvard Extension Alumni Symposium, and in Seattle at Mercer Street Books and The Grocery Studios. He is also a contributor to *Seattle Review of Books*.

www.ingramcontent.com/pod-product-compliance
Lightning Source LLC
Chambersburg PA
CBHW052052070526
44584CB00017B/2140